CH00852901

'My mind floo
Oh those cherisi
That have seare
Becoming part
Time after tim(

(Harrison Stickle.)

John Phoenix Hutchinson fell in love with the Lake District fells at a very young age and has completed the Wainwrights, being in his younger days a keen peak bagger! Now living and working in the Lake District John can often be seen up on the heights when time and condition allows.

Follow my Lake District adventures on line at
https://www.wainwrights-in-verse.com

John Phoenix Hutchinson © 2014
Second Edition 2015
The ISBN 10 assigned to this book is 1507852576
' and the ISBN 13 is 9781507852576

All poems are the work of John Phoenix Hutchinson © 2014

Cover picture of Harrison Stickle from Elterwater is reproduced here by kind permission of Keith Greenough © 2012.

Haystacks Publications ©2015

Introduction

Can you write a different mountain poem for 214 fells in the English Lake District without them all sounding marvellous mountain this or fabulous fell that?

The answer is a resounding yes, as hopefully this collection shows with each of the fells having very much its own character, from the fair foothills to the heights of the strong giants.

Thanks to the fabulous Alfred Wainwright guidebooks we now have a standardised list for our adventures. There are of course many more fells, especially in the outlying areas, but for the purposes here, I have stuck to the 214 Wainwrights, as they have become rightly known.

It took me twelve months on and off to write the poems; some are short and sweet, others long. I composed the majority in rhyme but not all. Some of the more moody mountains, as I call them, needed a more dark approach. Blencathra and the Sharp Edge ascent comes to mind.

I have listed them all alphabetically but each fell also has its own recognised region of North, North West, Central, East, Far East, South and West listed. Along with this I have written a brief introduction including the map coordinates (OS Grid) with height in the more traditional and grander total measure of feet! I have also given an indication of the quality of the summit views.

Some of my poems will tell you about a particular route, some have a more general summary, while others are inclined to have a more romantic or spiritual take. All combine to make what is hopefully an interesting mix that could be used as a literal introduction to a particular fell or perhaps also as an aid to reminisce about a wonderful adventure. Never should this guide be used purely on its own to walk the fells.

On that note, remember that the mountains whilst fun can be dangerous places. You should go correctly equipped with a good pair of walking boots, map and compass too, and know how to use them! In your rucksack have waterproofs, spare clothing, food and drink. Never walk or scramble up rock where you feel out of your comfort zone, but trust your instincts and in most cases the map.

The weather can be random even on a sunny day, changing for the worse dramatically, so be prepared to retreat in the face of adversity. I remember enjoying the sun one July on top of Bowfell. The wind got up, bringing clouds quickly from the western coastline and stinging hail rained down on me for twenty minutes before summer returned.

One last note: many place names are duplicated in the Lake District. I won't go into them all here but you will notice that in this book there are two of each Red Pike, Harter Fell and High Raise mountains. Thankfully most of these are found in very different regions with the one exception of the Red Pikes but this really is another reason to be familiar with the map.

I hope you enjoy the poetry, which was born of my love of the lakes. I am not the first to have experienced this calling and won't be the last to be endeared by the incredible beauty on display.

May the sun shine on your adventures here, but this being the English Lake District I make no promises whatsoever with regard to the weather! – John Phoenix Hutchinson.

ALLEN CRAGS

Region: South **Height:** 2,572 ft **Grid Ref:** NY237085

Part of the Scafell range of mountains, this fell is craggy and rocky, and falls away steeply to the head of the Langstrath valley on its eastern side, while its less steep western flanks are characterised by grey slabs of rock. Often traversed on the way to Scafell Pike the summit is well worth a visit especially for the grand view of Great Gable.

In the heart of the peaks you stand,
Intimate with famous forthright fells,
Rarely visited despite your merits many,
Though often seen as walkers pass you by,
Intent on loftier heights despite your size.

A refuge, a sanctuary from busier paths,
Not so scarred by footfalls heavy graft,
The view although in shadowed walls,
Frames Lakeland's pleasant picture,
Of precious tarns and rocky vista.

ANGLETARN PIKES

Region: Far East **Height:** 1,857 ft **Grid Ref:** NY413148

Often climbed from near Patterdale village, Angletarn Pikes stands on the western arm of a long horseshoe ridge which surrounds the Martindale valley system, which heads north and drains into beautiful Ullswater. Angle Tarn itself is a delightful water hidden high amongst the fells. There are two summits here hence the "pikes" name, the northern one being the true summit. Views from both are really good, especially of Helvellyn.

Enigmatic twofold summit surprises,
For sheer slopes stealthy hide this,
Nestled into shoulder lovingly reclined,
Angle Tarn waters beauty defined,
Peace and love will come ardent to fore,
Along one of Lakeland's best loved shores.

ARD CRAGS

Region: North West **Height:** 1,906 ft **Grid Ref:** NY207198

Ard Crags is situated close to other higher fells such as Causey Pike and Eel Crag and can be easily overlooked as it is situated up a minor road along the Newlands valley. Pyramidal in shape when seen from certain angles, the sweeping ridge is lovely to roam along and although the view from here is restricted by higher fells, the Newlands valley is well seen below.

Low-level bracken,
High-level heather,
One of those fine fells,
Best in summer weather.

For August highlights,
So soft springy carpet,
Famous Rigg Beck walk,
Most fun fulfilling target.

ARMBOTH FELL

Region: Central **Height:** 1,572 ft **Grid Ref:** NY297159

Most paths lead up from Thirlmere, with the slopes on the lakeside being very interesting with some great water features. The summit sadly is not so exciting being set in a depression which collects water all year round from higher fells so is very wet underfoot to say the least. The best views are not seen from here but try Fisher Crag for a good view of the lake.

Although summit of Armboth is wasteland,
A wet mossy swamp, so tread with care,
On western dark wooded fringe of water,
Lies a trail of wild nature most fair.

For on tracks that lead up glistening gills,
You will find hidden beauty abounds,
The falls of Launchy are quite outstanding,
As are views from Fisher Crag of Thirlmere sound.

ARNISON CRAG

Region: East **Height:** 1,421 ft **Grid Ref:** NY393150

Arnison Crag is a lower subsidiary ridge of Birks which itself leads to St Sunday Crag. The fell is a low rock tower which can be distinctively seen from surrounding valleys. Here from this perch, an interesting view of the lake comes into view.

> The Patterdale path you joyfully take,
> That view's grand lauded so loved lake,
> Here crags fall down, curved round bend,
> On Deepdale grass shelf lower end,
> Just a short step from here to tower heights,
> This after lunch stroll enjoys Ullswater delights.

ARTHUR'S PIKE

Region: Far East **Height:** 1,749 ft **Grid Ref:** NY461206

Most visitors to this area arrive by the Ullswater ferry or along ways from Pooley Bridge. The summit – a grass topped plateau – is in complete contrast to its more imposing lakeside craggy face where good views of Ullswater can be seen.

> The fell fringe flatters to deceive,
> As forbidding flanks are perceived,
> Easy Howtown path the route to go,
> From the ferry many footsteps freely flow.
>
> Soon a tricky tempting place can be seen,
> The rockwalls Swarthbeck Gill ravine,
> NOT the pedestrian way to height,
> Only strong climbers, scramblers here fight.

BAKESTALL

Region: North **Height:** 2,208 ft **Grid Ref:** NY266307

North of the town of Keswick this slate mountain is famous for the imposing cleft of Dead Crags and Dash Beck waterfalls. The view from the summit is curtailed by other mountains, especially Skiddaw. However, you can get a good glimpse of the Solway Firth and the Scottish Hills from here.

Dark shadows in Dead Crags hollow,
Though dark shades of life prevail,
Bilberry greens, ling purple browns,
Lend colour to broken rim and rampart.

Hark the sound of War! Where white water roars,
The mighty torrents thrash, crystals crash,
And thunder sounds beneath the shaking ground,
In deep wooded ravine, lauded Dash Falls scene.

BANNERDALE CRAGS

Region: North **Height:** 2,241 ft **Grid Ref:** NY335290

Steep-sided crags abound when seen from Munsgrisdale Common making this fell best climbed from Mungrisdale village. The top is smooth in comparison with a surprisingly good view. You can ride up and down the grassy saddle ridge to Bowscale Fell.

In Bannerdale old lead mine lands,
The ridge rises to eastern stand,
Here rim escarpment rides erratic waves,
Sloping gently down on grassy blades,
Stark contrast to arising arresting face,
Crags crashing down with deadly pace.

BARF

Region: North West **Height:** 1,535 ft **Grid Ref:** NY216267

This popular fell, a subsidiary of Lord's Seat, has a famous white painted stone feature at 700 feet that can be seen from the road. Called the Bishop of Barf, a local legend says that the Bishop of Derry (1783) was killed here riding his horse up the mountain face! Both the Bishop and poor horse are said to be buried near or under the so-called Clerk at the base. The fell itself is a really steep graded "scramble" when tackled head on and this route is described in the poem. However, there is an easier "walk" via Beckstones Gill. The summit provides excellent views of Skiddaw and Longside Edge.

All pilgrims assemble, check in with the Clerk,
For the enterprise ahead is short but stiff work,
Here lies a quest, a climbing crusade,
That the Bishop above so proudly displays.

The scramble up mountain, a steep raise and reach,
Grand words from the pulpit his worship doth preach,
Not for the fragile, faint heart or weak,
Only those with vigour and strength do we seek.

Fight through bracken, thick gorse and scree,
Watch out for loose rock, the slate is slippy,
Force your way up gully, traverse Slape Crag too,
False prophets will fool you before Barf baptises you.

BARROW

Region: North West **Height:** 1,493 ft **Grid Ref:** NY226218

A rewarding ramble from Braithwaite, up either of the two paths from there. An easy fell of no great height but more than worth the short climb for the views which are really good, especially towards the Derwentwater.

From Braithwaite foot Barrow gives birth,
Gentle rising ridge, broad flanks show worth,
Mined at heart, scars show the deep pain,
Now mellowed by nature and kiss of the rain,
Third class in height, first class the view,
Glorious grand vista, Derwentwater protrudes.

BASE BROWN

Region: West **Height:** 2,119 ft **Grid Ref:** NY225114

Base Brown is situated in the upper reaches of Borrowdale and here begins an area of rough and rugged rock. Often visited on the way to Great Gable the view from the summit is restricted by higher mountains but the fell is still is worth a visit to see the Scafell range close up.

Stark striking fells of western station,
Begin with Base Brown wild desolation,
Gaunt ruination, fertile pastures forsaken,
Drama of Hanging Stone, steep declination.

To climb a mountain you must have the will,
And water lends strength in Sour Milk Gill,
Beautiful stream, breaks, cascades, falls,
Feeding River Derwent young adolescent calls.

BEDA FELL

Region: Far East **Height:** 1,670 ft **Grid Ref:** NY427171

This fell is easily climbed from the enclosed Howtown road and the finger ridge can be walked without too much drama in a gradual ascent all the way to Angletarn Pikes. The view is good of the surrounding fells and Ullswater is glimpsed either side of Hallin Fell.

Deep elegant valleys delineate, define,
The broad long body of ridge, riding,
Reaching out, descending, narrowing,
Pointing, showing the paths that lay
The hidden heart of Ullswater sway.

BINSEY

Region: North **Height:** 1,467 ft **Grid Ref:** NY225355

Binsey is bit of an odd one out being detached from the rest of the Lakeland fells and standing in a low level watershed. It provides though an excellent viewpoint of the Northern and North Western fells you'll find hard to match. This pudding basin is climbed with little effort being gentle in slope and height and is the perfect spot for an old school picnic.

Solitary station stands alone,
Sunday stroll, a gentle roam,
More than worthy of your presence,
Unrestricted panorama impeccably present,
Bask in the sun or dance in the rain,
Binsey brings only joys, no banes.

BIRKHOUSE MOOR

Region: East **Height:** 2,356 ft **Grid Ref:** NY364160

Birkhouse Moor often acts as a staging post to the ascent of Helvellyn from Patterdale village or Glenridding. A sweeping grassy-topped plateau ridge makes its way to one of the most famous places in the Lakes – Striding Edge. At Keldas, the wooded area overlooking the lake, many photographs have been taken and pictures painted as the view of the water through the firs is of the finest quality.

A swathe of verdant grass parades
On top of sprawling promenade,
And windswept blades all spiral round,
The patterns sweep along the ground.

Till eastern slope descends off moor,
At Keldas wooded Lakeland door,
Such is the scene from this grand place,
Where Lanty's Tarn view embraces grace.

BIRKS

Region: East **Height:** 2,041 ft **Grid Ref:** NY380143

Usually climbed from Patterdale on route to its grander parent fell St Sunday Crag. Most guidebooks will tell you that the fell is of little merit and whilst I can sympathise with that, I find it hard to be disparaging of anywhere in the Lakes. Birks certainly has some merit, especially as a good viewpoint of lower Ullswater. It is a very easy summit to attain quickly via the route in the poem.

From Grisedale Beck Ascend! Ascend!
Above the wall on Thornhow End,
Up steep slope aside Black Crag,
You'll arrive at Birks,
With summit bagged.

BLACK FELL

Region: South **Height:** 1,060 ft **Grid Ref:** NY341016

Although modest in height Black Fell stands pivotal in the Lake District being bounded by Windermere, Langdale and Coniston. Beatrix Potter owned the fell at one time before handing it on to all of us via the National Trust. Trees cover the lower slopes but the summit is clear and Windermere can be seen. The low southern slopes are outstanding in beauty and many people make a beeline for Tarn Hows.

Alone from woodlands you steeply climb,
Clothed in bracken's dense dark weave,
Your Tarn Hows view so loved and popular,
Its charmed beauty Man conceived.

Standing fine heading from the west,
Shining Windermere comes into view,
And prominent peaks of Langdale heights,
That adventurers' hearts doth woo.

BLAKE FELL

Region: Western **Height:** 1880 ft **Grid Ref:** NY110196

Blake Fell sits above Loweswater on the northern arm of the Western fells. Although modest in height the long finger ridge is dominant in this region, the varying tops of which have many names. The main summit view is a grand one, especially westward towards the sea and for a good view of Crummock Water head along to Loweswater End.

Mightiest of Loweswater fells,
Splendid panorama inland tells,
Skiddaw, Blencathra, Helvellyn too,
Great End, Pillar and Scafell viewed.
Seaward the scene undoubtedly thrills,
West Cumberland unveiled up to Scottish hills

BLEA RIGG

Region: Central **Height:** 1,775 ft **Grid Ref:** NY302078

Many pictures are taken from Blea Rigg but not of the fell itself. This is down to its excellent points of special view, especially in the shape of Easedale Tarn near Grasmere and Pavey Ark in Langdale. This fell puts on its best show on the Grasmere side with a dark craggy face. The ridge can be climbed from many starting points with Silver How a popular route.

A mountain that shows most intimate face,
High above Easedale Tarn's tranquil grace,
The contrast of beauty before the beast,
As crags fall down in grand boulder feast.

From Sergeant Man to Silver How,
And Dungeon Ghyll to Grasmere crowd,
The many throng along the rocky routes,
In waterproof jackets and well-worn boots.

BLEABERRY FELL

Region: Central **Height:** 1,936 ft **Grid Ref:** NY285195

Bleaberry is a fine central standpoint although it is not exciting from the point of having rough and rugged rock, being for the most part gentle and heather clad. The view is of the highest grade and although not the best vista of them all, it is certainly very much premier league Lakeland fayre including all the major fell groups. The bonus view of Derwentwater can be seen from the north-west summit cairn.

Dont forget the camera!
Advice I've given you should firmly trust,
For when I type it in italics,
It certainly is a must.

Though Bleaberry is no classic fell,
Its fine standpoint I declare divine,
Magnificent sweeping summit panorama,
To close your eyes would be a crime.

Breathe deeply as you take show in,
Mountain air, accentuated by sweet scent,
The short springy heather trod underfoot,
Is a joy you will find heaven sent.

BLENCATHRA

Region: North Height: 2,848 ft Grid Ref: NY323277

If you have a good head for heights, which hopefully you do seeing as you're reading a book about mountains, then out of the hundreds of ascents up the ever popular Blencathra I can thoroughly recommend the one that goes by way of Sharp Edge alluded to in the poem. This is a scramble up a razor-edged arête that compares in exhilaration to that of Striding Edge on Helvellyn, and neither should be missed. Those not keen on a bit of exposure should try the easier but still excellent ascent from Thelkeld via Halls Fell. Blencathra is a serious broad mountain landscape with no less than six separate fell tops. Don't forget the map, compass and waterproofs. The weather up here can be especially harsh, so beware of strong winds and sudden sharp falling slopes. This is not a place to get lost.

Darkness looms on black broken horizon,
Unforgiving, uninviting, menacing, shadow mass,
Sinister presence prevails, threatening,
Ominous airs, cruel winds with brutal tempers,
Riding fast then faster, whipped hard,
Round intimidating, enclosing, shattered walls,
Rivers of violent rock and stone,
Bleak desolation where you stand alone,
So very alone as proximity gives panic,
As towers close in dangerous prospect,
You dare risk the vengeance,
The retribution...you are tested!
The sharp edge...the ultimatum.

BONSCALE PIKE

Region: Far East **Height:** 1,719 ft **Grid Ref:** NY453201

Bonscale Pike sits above Howtown on Ullswater and the view of the Helvellyn range across the lake is a grand one. The pike itself is a grassy spur running down from Loadpot Hill. As they pull up to the pier, passengers on the lake steamer will really notice the western crags, near where a popular path slants up the breast of the fell.

Broad buttress and dark defensive rim,
Protecting Howtown or fencing it in?
The top pillar views, undeniable in grace,
Especially towards high Helvellyn face,
Across the lake you'll look for a long while,
The unfolding view sweeps many a mile.

BOWFELL

Region: South **Height:** 2,959 ft **Grid Ref:** NY245064

A very much loved mountain and firm favourite amongst experienced Lakeland journeymen and day trippers alike. There are so many interesting rock features to discover here and the quality of the neighbouring mountains and wide valleys adds to the fantastic views all round. There are many great ways to ascend Bowfell, but for me approaching it via Crinkle Crags and then taking the Climbers Traverse to the summit rather than the main well-worn path is a real delight, the latter part being a tiring but unexposed scramble to the top taking in the famous Great Slab.

Oh Bowfell your grand stature,
Demands the greatest reflect,
Admiration shown to your prominence,
A rugged beauty to show due respect.

So many joys you deliver proudly,
I will list my firm favourites first,
God's cut with knife at Great Slab,
Wondrous hidden Climbers' Traverse.

Flat Crags is decorated with climbers,
And Cambridge has the best drink,
The Bowfell Buttress is quite beautiful,
North Gully should make you think.

Three Tarns really is an enigma,
When last was there it had five?
A meeting point from Crinkle Crags,
The direct route here it thrives.

The Band it is well trodden,
Fastest way up or down,
Your summit is always busy,
Like it has a human crown.

Your neighbours are most worthy,
And joy they bring of their own,
From Bowfell top you see many,
Another great adventure shown.

BOWSCALE FELL

Region: North **Height:** 2,303 ft **Grid Ref:** NY334305

The tarn on Bowscale Fell is one of the best in the district and in its heyday was visited by thousands of Victorians who rode to the waters on pack ponies. Nowadays it's not so busy and you have to make your way there on foot with most ascents starting from Mungrisdale Village. The view from the top of nearby Blencathra and Sharp Edge is awesome.

Glacial scene at silent waters,
Home of immortal fish yarn,
Here solitude and romance,
Can be found at Bowscale Tarn.

For one of the fish has the power of speech!
And will quietly give grand greetings to you,
"Hello and welcome to this wild watery waste,
Where I study the clouds and sky blue."

BRAE FELL

Region: North **Height:** 1,923 ft **Grid Ref:** NY288351

Brae Fell, the last northerly fell of Lakeland, is a bit plain looks-wise when compared to a multitude of others. However, from its summit is seen a fine view of the Solway Firth, the Scottish Hills and the Northern Pennines. Easily climbed from a minor road along its length, although paths can be a bit indistinct in the grass, it is not difficult to find a way to the top. On its eastern side are spoil heaps from an old Victorian lead mine.

Last outpost of Lakeland North,
More grass than rock here springs forth,
Long ago drift mines once here worked,
Broken, disguised, the remnants now lurk,
Rich yield of ores, mine harvested at pace,
Though mountain is bland its view no disgrace.

BRANDRETH

Region: West **Height:** 2,346 ft **Grid Ref:** NY215119

Often climbed on the way to Great Gable the summit is rocky flat ground and a rather bleak place. The view ahead though is the main destination of the many visitors to Brandreth and the grand dome of Great Gable speaks for itself. Many climb this way via Honister Mine because of the high- level head start but other paths that lead up from Gatesgarth and Borrowdale are more than worthy.

Desolate desert of stones,
Chilled winds cut to the bones,
Brandreth plateau a regular staple,
On route to grander Great Gable,
Broad western valley view displayed here,
Commanding joys of Ennerdale and Buttermere.

BRANSTREE

Region: Far East **Height:** 2,339 ft **Grid Ref:** NY477100

Branstree is one of a circuit of high fells round Mardale, where rough grass and moorland prevail on this infrequently used approach to High Street and the Roman road. The falls from Hopgill Beck are a "must visit" in an area which lacks features. A huge, very long pipe tunnel was mined through this mountain to supply water to the big cities.

To survey from Branstree is a feat,
For summit runs broad to old High Street,
Grass swathe and moor run cross ridge bands,
Lookout for the sharp steep falls in Hopgill land,
Tarn Crag and Great Howe carry hidden pipe,
A fresh drink for Manchester, Haweswater type.

BRIM FELL

Region: South **Height:** 2,612 ft **Grid Ref:** SD271986

One does not waltz straight up Brim Fell in a hurry although it can be done with care. Most will traverse the summit via Coniston Old Man or Swirl How when walking the main ridge, which is a grand enterprise in itself. There is plenty of evidence of mining operations in this region and care should always be taken when exploring them. The views are really good from here, if slightly restricted in the foreground because of the mountain's broad convex shape.

The Old Man's whaleback brother,
So ungainly craggy roughly faced,
Tempered by grassy high pass,
Almost strangely out of place.

From Levers Water to the Hause,
With mining scars and boulder stairs,
Stark buttress of the Raven Tor,
A combination of the grim and fair.

BROCK CRAGS

Region: Far East **Height:** 1,844 ft **Grid Ref:** NY419137

High above Hartsop village a narrow climbing ridge heading eastwards can be seen. Brock Crags provides a really great platform for viewing all round in this area and easy ascents can be made from the village. Higher up, paths become unclear so head towards the two highest knolls keeping your eye out for a small tarn in between.

Your humble poet has a favoured place,
For at Brothers Water I've often graced,
The view of which is so grandly seen,
From Brock Crags summit so serene.

Hartsop or Patterdale paths you'll climb,
Passing by gill and wooded reclines,
Eagerly exploring nature's finest ways,
Meeting your fellows and bidding Good Day.

BROOM FELL

Region: North West **Height:** 1.677 ft **Grid Ref:** NY195271

If you are a summit bagger this place is a must otherwise if am honest it is rarely climbed. Broom Fell really does not compare to the more exciting places in this region although for me every place in the Lakes has its own individual charms and if you like regimented woodland and mossy swamps as in the form of Wythop Moss you'll be in your element here. The view from the summit isn't half bad with the coastal plain and the Solway Firth making a fine vista.

Broad Broom round,
Grass height bland,
Valleys organised timbers,
Wythop Moss hinders,
Old path history,
Dry footed mystery.

BUCKBARROW

Region: West **Height:** 1,388 ft **Grid Ref:** NY135061

When seen from the minor road at its base Buckbarrow can look unassailable and the front crags are strictly the playground of climbers. You can scramble to the rocky base of these crags for closer inspection but the main walkers' path sets out from Harrow Head Farm. A great view of Wastwater can be seen from the summit along with from the main crag.

Cheerful and charming to clamber,
Bold rock full front need not hamper,
For Gill Beck lies on a well beaten track,
That easily lets you roam freely round back,
From Pike Crag and summit it's easy to see,
The length of the deep lake at Wastwater Screes.

BURNBANK FELL

Region: West Height: 1,558 ft Grid Ref: NY110209

One of the lower fells surrounding Loweswater, where pleasant paths can be found along the lake shore that lead into the wood and onto the terrace above the tree line. A pair of waterfalls in the wood are the real highlight for many. The view of Lakeland from the summit is hidden by Blake Fell but the coastal sights are worth the trip there.

**Hudson Place Farm for Waterend,
A gentle stroll that joyfully sends,
Amongst the wood there is a course,
Serenading sequence called Holme Force,
Procession of falls and sylvan dreams,
Set below fell with seaward scenes.**

CALF CRAG

Region: Central Height: 1,762 ft Grid Ref: NY302105

Calf Crag is often indirectly ascended as part of the Greenburn Horseshoe route. The ground around the base, especially in Wythburn valley, is very boggy and you might have to jump around a bit to avoid the worst bits. Although this is a wet country area I found it to be full of interest with a certain beauty of its own. The summit view is very restricted by higher fells but Grasmere and Helvellyn are seen to great effect.

**Three valleys of beautiful rugged rocky waste,
Far Easedale, Greenburn, Wythburn at base,
Wonderful watershed of central Lakeland fells,
Dale adventures will leave you with tales to tell,
No calfs on this crag though flow flocks of sheep,
Look out for droppings, there's plenty in heaps!**

CARL SIDE

Region: North **Height:** 2,448 ft **Grid Ref:** NY255280

Carl Side is one of the Skiddaw family of fells and although it can be ascended in its own right, it is often climbed on the way to Skiddaw itself. The summit, a grassy plateau, is an excellent platform for views of Derwentwater. The fell can be ascended from many places but the shortest starting point and most popular route is given in the poem.

Ride the grass-topped saddle to Skiddaw,
Presenting path from Millbeck no hard chore
Though sudden cliffs on Doups a right real surprise,
Quartz White Stones here, brashly boldly bright lies.

Watch out for sharp arête, striated soaring rocks,
That lie on heather south ridge way to tallest top,
Southern vista opens out on wide waters call,
Northern mountains ahead, stand towering tall.

CARROCK FELL

Region: North **Height:** 2,169 ft **Grid Ref:** NY341336

As mountains go Carrock Fell is famous on three fronts: its geology, its mines and most of all its Iron Age hill fort on its summit. This was thought to have stood till the Romans attacked the fort during the conquest of Britain and remains can still be seen and traced out on the ground today. The unique geology here brought the miners for centuries, seeking tungsten, lead, arsenic and iron, with the last mine closing in 1980.

Turn back the tides of time to ancient man, imagine,
Imagine the laborious effort, toil and the sweat,
To raise the circled walls, the rocky ramparts
For tribal defence in the cold and the wet.

Envisage fortifications now foundered succumbed to ages,
Standing firm against wind and hand of man,
A last strong defence, an enduring refuge,
And sheltered home in wild and savage land.

Who lies silent under raised earth?
Long dead fallen warrior? Valiant King?
Honoured leader of mountain country,
Did he fight the good fight? Lose or Win?

CASTLE CRAG

Region: North West **Height:** 951 ft **Grid Ref:** NY249159

Castle Crag is not the grandest height – it is in fact the smallest listed here. But do not let that put you off a visit to this place as it is one of the most unique and interesting environments to investigate. The walk to the summit from Derwentwater is a grand adventure and a fine valley view displays.

Short scally scamp, rugged redoubt,
Despite small stature a magnificent mount,
So full of character, eccentric unique
From steep sided summit to Borrowdale feet,

Derwent River flows beneath the silvered grooves
And the quarries that you find are the secrets of the mines,
Bare naked rock, precipitous dangers drop, drop, drop,
Here all combine sublime, sylvan Castle Crag defined.

CATBELLS

Region: North West **Height:** 1,480 ft **Grid Ref:** NY244199

The day trippers' delight for visitors to Keswick and scene of many a postcard, Catbells is easy to climb with well-established paths and can be combined with a trip on the ferry to make for a perfect Lakeland adventure. Views on the walk up and from the summit are outstanding and its low height makes it attainable in half a day, leaving the rest of the time for a glorious picnic on this well-loved fell.

Catbells draws souls across the mirror lake
With the mystical magic only Cumbria makes,
Sleek sultry slopes boldly define,
Famous flowing smooth skyward outlines,
The journey is easy, open to one and all,
Beware though old mine shafts with deadly falls,
Reward of summit stairway, paradise, bliss,
Viewed from above untold beauty God gives.

CATSTYCAM

Region: East **Height:** 2,920 ft **Grid Ref:** NY348158

A lofty imposing satellite of Helvellyn attached via the semi-famous arête of Swirral Edge. When seen on ascents from Glenridding the mountain takes the form of a near perfect pyramid so is easy to identify. Often climbed on the way down from Helvellyn it makes up part of the circular tour that I would rank as one of the best walks in the Lake District, if not the whole country, starting at Birkhouse Moor and heading along Striding Edge up to Helvellyn. Despite being hemmed in by Helvellyn and Birkhouse Moor the summit gives close views of the joys mentioned.

**Your simple sharp soaring lines,
Curvature culminating supreme,
Peaked prominence piercing sky,
Of all glorious mountain forms
Catstycam – so near perfection.**

CAUDALE MOOR

Region: Far East **Height:** 2,503 ft **Grid Ref:** NY417100

The mountain of many names but I am an old traditionalist and stick with Wainwright's Caudale Moor and seeing as we are using his list of mountains it would be rude not to, me thinks. This fell can be climbed from the top of Kirkstone Pass but really that's cheating! Besides, the most rewarding paths start from Patterdale and climb to the three summits. Here you can scramble down to the Kirkstone Inn at the top of the pass via St Raven's Edge for a well-earned beer – but not before! Up top many ridge ways head in all directions so, as always, remember the map and compass. The view is good if a little restricted by a flat summit and the closeness of other fells.

**Six ridge ways off Caudale Moor,
Confusion with names is also in store,
For sometimes called Stony Cove Pike,
Or John Bell's Banner the one I like,
Easily climbed from the Kirkstone Inn
Not starting from Brothers Water is truly a sin!**

CAUSEY PIKE

Region: North West **Height:** 2,090 ft **Grid Ref:** NY218208

Causey Pike is easily recognisable as its distinctive mole-like humps sticks out for miles around. Often climbed as part of the Coledale Round its scree slopes yield the occasional fossil. The ascent from the Newlands valley is a steep one with the last hundred feet or so a rocky but worthwhile scramble. The narrow ridge summit rewards your efforts to conquer with a most excellent view. The annual fell race here is run in March and climbs 1800 feet which the winners do in just over thirty minutes! It is fun to watch and good luck to them, but I will stick to the walking.

**Direct route taken from foot of Newlands Stair,
Ellas Crag, Rowling End, Sleet Hause fair,
Here the tower suddenly rises, hands firmly hit rock,
Strange shape of Causey Pike all eyes the target locked,
Up and down the pointed narrow range ridge runs,
Survey the beauty with the windy heights duly won.**

CAW FELL

Region: West **Height:** 2,287 ft **Grid Ref:** NY132109

Caw Fell is one of the most westerly from central Lakeland, so is a remote solitary place but a beautiful one and worthy of a visit with the bonus of the unhindered view. There is some evidence of mining from Victorian times, a failed venture as the iron ore was of a low grade though they tried for over thirty years. Evidence can also be seen on the northern face of glacial drift and the area of Stockdale Moor on the lower slope is full of the signs of ancient man with raised earthworks and enclosed circles.

**Wide green grass pastures slope to sea,
Miles of smooth rolling heights to lonely be,
No more amiable mountain are you likely to meet,
Than to have gentle, graceful Caw beneath your feet,
By the summit wall you will silently, soulfully stand,
Studying the lordly might of the wide western band.**

CLOUGH HEAD

Region: East **Height:** 2,382 ft **Grid Ref:** NY333225

Clough Head is the most northerly tip of the Helvellyn range and the fell itself is full of interest. There was a lot of mining activity here, (the Threlkeld Mining Museum is worth a visit), also the Romano British had a large settlement on its slopes nearby and enclosure walls can easily be seen. The view without doubt is most excellent from the summit, with the Western fells really showing their worth. The craggy Western face of the fell has one breach called Fisher's Wife's Rake but this is for competent scramblers "ascending" only and not for the average walker.

Inquisitive mind on Clough Head thrives,
For curiosity here well told is truly alive,
Many quarries line along craggy western face,
From aged old coach road pick up that pace.
And head towards the past, ancient antique bounds,
Iron Age settlement placed here on the ground.

Continue to climb the climax, endmost fell,
Head towards gate and surprising Hause Well,
Puzzling fresh spring within these rigid rocks,
Now onto White Pike the carrion birds here flock,
Riding on easterly winds and soaring so so high,
The summit not now far on the crisp horizon sky.

COLD PIKE

Region: South Height: 2,300 ft Grid Ref: NY262035

Cold Pike is one of those summits sadly often missed as walkers make a beeline for Crinkle Crags. This is a shame as the view from here is really quite stunning, not just because of the close proximity of the aforementioned but the Langdale Pikes and the far end of the Coniston range across Wrynose Pass also put on a grand show. A glimpse of the Pennines, Morecambe Bay and Windermere add to the scene. Red Tarn, which is also nearby, is not the prettiest of waters as Lakeland tarns go but makes a good focal point for the main paths hereabouts.

Cold Pike, Cold Pike, I love you so,
Though not many people here will flow,
Greater significance given to your friends,
Your three summits soulful solitude can lend,
Extensive northeasterly principal views,
Studied in silence from rocky church pews.

CONISTON OLD MAN

Region: South Height: 2,634 ft Grid Ref: SD272978

The history of Coniston Old Man is in little doubt with mining and farming taking part on its slopes for over a thousand years and before. The mountain has yielded much copper and slate, the latter continuing today. The fellside is heavily scarred and many old openings and shafts can be discovered round the profusion of old workings and slag heaps, but none should be entered! Up to ten flocks of sheep, sometimes more, graze on its slopes so one would never be lonely walking here. They are so used to seeing the profusion of tourists that they are quite tame and know that unattended rucksacks often have sandwiches for them with those that live near the summit especially so! On more than one occasion I have seen unsuspecting walkers cunningly "stalked" and their lunch stolen by a hit and run raid.

The Old Man of Coniston bears many scars,
Centuries abused by grasping hand of man,
To respect this benevolent giant is a duty,
For even in ugliness lies greater beauty.

Bared to the bones, shredding deep pools of tears,
Born in the clouds sustained in the mist,
The dignified geography loved in affinity,
The village, lake, mountain in glorious trinity.

Copper, slate, slag devastation rudely prevails,
From his broad feet to platform summit,
Proud and venerable features give ancient raise,
Mined valleys, dangerous shafts, where no sheep graze.
The waters, the falls, are a regular pilgrimage,
To glacial destruction that rivals man's ruination,
So many treasures in fern, bracken and heather,
So many discoveries awaiting your endeavour.

CRAG FELL

Region: West Height: 1,175 ft Grid Ref: NY079194

Crag Fell overlooks Ennerdale Water, a very popular lake for anglers, with its relative remoteness from central Lakeland, away from the tourists being a draw, as well as the good fishing to be had here. The most interesting path is along the shore line in front of the fell till you get to the crag, from where a path works its way up the fell. En route you will pass some very interesting 80-foot splinters of rock rising above the slope. There are some fair views from the summit although you are reminded of the harsher realities of life in the form of the Sellafield nuclear power station visible on the coastline.

Where rocks plunge, plummet then falter,
At fisherman's lake they call Ennerdale Water,
Here you'll find some curious standing pinnacles,
The creation of which is a geological miracle,
Head up past waterside to prominent Anglers' Crag,
Revelin Crag displays proudly before summit you bag.

CRINKLE CRAGS

Region: South **Height:** 2,818 ft **Grid Ref:** NY248048

Crinkle Crags is without doubt one of the best ridge walks you can do in Lakeland. It's not just the mountain itself that makes it so but the wonderful views that unfold and display as you make your way up and down the adventure that is the five crinkles. Along the ridge, the notorious Bad Step, a short but steep cleft with a chockstone, can be easily bypassed or with some help conquered! I can say hand on heart that this fell is exhilarating and very highly recommended, but make sure it's a fine day as you would not want to get lost in the mist here and not to see the panorama would be a shame.

Crinkle Crags takes off its cloudy crown,
Revealing in golden sunlight's breaking rays,
Unmistakable undulations in rugged desolation,
Step serrated crags, gaunt gullies in depression,
A dramatic delight flourishing in procession.

Wild! Ruination, a raging mountain's mountain,
A hokey cokey dance set in rock and stone,
A conga of ridges in rhythmic flows,
Bestowing a musical extravaganza in lofty place,
A crazy madcap song performed at breakneck pace.

Beware though its joys, explore with a caution,
To the unwary, the crags make many fools in pathless mist,
Jesters of the steep shattered slippery scree,
For valours best side should be shown due respect,
Most especially in chockstone gullies like the Bad Step.

DALE HEAD

Region: North West **Height:** 2,470 ft **Grid Ref:** NY223153

Dale Head is one of those mountains situated near a high road, or in this case the top of Honister Pass. Personally, I see this as cheating but sometimes it just has to be done when the best approach is from that direction. The ways up from the Newlands and Borrowdale valleys certainly have merit, especially the latter via Launchy Tarn. The fell itself has a mining history going back to Tudor times that ended in the 1960s. Originally mined for pyrites, over the years emphasis shifted to Cumbrian green slate. The mountain has a lot of character from top to bottom and is well worthy of a visit with great views pretty much all round.

Dark hidden shades and secret shadows,
Ancient workings long departed hallows,
Abandoned mines profusely litter the scene,
Centuries old routes where miners' feet have been,
Nook, rigg and pillar, bold rock, scattered scree,
Make Dale Head Mountain a real must see.

DODD

Region: North **Height:** 1,647 ft **Grid Ref:** NY244273

This popular little fell is just north of Keswick, and has become well known for its rarer wildlife that includes a pair of nesting ospreys and red squirrels. There are a myriad of paths to get lost on in the heavily wooded slopes. The summit over recent years has had a programme of deforestation carried out, opening up the excellent view of Derwentwater. Adventures normally start from the Old Sawmill Tearoom along the A591 road and can be continued from here all the way to the lofty heights of Skiddaw itself.

Let's play a game, a puzzle to solve,
Enter the labyrinth, the woodland soul,
Larch, spruce, fir, pine, bar your way,
The wood pigeons talk, they have their say,
"Why are they lost, cannot they find
Roads to the summit, paths in a line?"

DOLLYWAGGON PIKE

Region: East **Height:** 2,815 ft **Grid Ref:** NY346130

Part of the southernmost tip of the Helvellyn range, and like most of the fells here, the western approaches of Dollywaggon Pike are grassy slopes, as opposed to the eastern sides where steep bare rock shows a proud and prominent front. Best climbed from Patterdale, paths head upwards to The Tongue and although this way provides a long ascent it is well worth the effort. The summit provides extensive views all round with the eastern aspect impressive. The famous Grisedale Tarn can be visited nearby, where tales tell of the last King of Cumbria, Dunmail, having his crown placed in the lake after battling both the English and Scottish Kings in AD 945.

No clue to the sheer violence bestowed,

On western green and gentle slopes.

No sign of complete carnage, devastation, desolation,

On easy pilgrims' path to much frequented heights.

No suggestion of the ferocity of nature's force,

On the eastern heavy scarred and damaged face.

The ravenous rent into your heart complete.

DOVE CRAG

Region: East Height: 2,598 ft Grid Ref: NY374104

Most people climb Dove Crag from Ambleside as part of the Fairfield Horseshoe walk but this does not take in the ascent from the lovely secluded valley of Dovedale, the route mentioned in my poem. Dovedale is not a place to miss with its unrivalled beauty, and the fell is best seen from this side to boot. Also on this face, near the heights, is a hidden cave I challenge you to find! The first chapter of the famous Alfred Wainwright guides was begun here in Dovedale with the 214 fells taking him fourteen years to complete – a grand work lovingly done and inspiration to many.

Dovedale is the best way to go,
The valley's lovely, the waters flow,
Slowly along this sylvan place,
As steepness increases so does its pace,
Crashing, crescendoing at Dove Falls,
Leave trees behind for rocky walls,
Along past The Stangs enter Hunsett Cove,
Hunt for Priest Hole hidden treasure trove,
Then moving onto tarn, last leg to heights,
Surrounded by mountains displaying their might.

DOW CRAG

Region: South **Height:** 2,552 ft **Grid Ref:** SD262977

Dow Crag is well known as a climbers' mountain due to the popularity of its buttressed face. There are now over a hundred recognised rock climbing routes here, most given names such as Giant's Crawl, Nimrod and the Shining Path. Walkers can gain the summit from the easy and popular way via Goat's Hause or by the much steeper scramble up the scree in South Gully. The summit, even in summer, is often cold and windy as it is very exposed. The views of Lakeland in the main are blocked by Coniston Old Man except to the south where water is very much the theme.

Grand words for a grand mountain,
Glorious in architectural grace,
Lauded by Lakeland's ancient cragsmen,
For the imposing magnificence of its face.

Towering tall above the stony hollow,
Exalted principal buttresses abound,
Multiplied by near vertical gullies,
Hallowed preserve rock climbing ground.

From the delectable exhilaration of the summit,
To the ever pleasant woods of Torver below,
There is no denying its cold hard beauty,
For on Dow Crag spirits soar and souls grow.

EAGLE CRAG

Region: Central **Height:** 1,709 ft **Grid Ref:** NY275121

Eagle Crag might look solely the premise of the rock climber but this impressive crag can be ascended safely by the average walker although because of the sudden dangerous drops, not seen from above, descent this way is not recommended and the well-worn path down Greenup Gill should be used. The crag is situated rather grandly where the Langstrath and Greenup valleys meet and is unmistakable from Stonethwaite. The sight from the summit along the valley is good with Borrowdale and associated fells coming into view. I didn't see any eagles up there but crows and ravens seemed to like the place.

At the base of Stonethwaite Beck's flow,
Look above to a proportioned plateau,
Such a sturdy prominence you never did see,
The playground of carrion, soaring happily.

Of the two routes to top one has a risk,
Don't even contemplate it in rain or a mist,
For tilted slabs of rock fall fast to the floor,
If you're stuck on the summit seek Greenup's back door.

EEL CRAG

Region: North West **Height:** 2,753 ft **Grid Ref:** NY192203

Marked now on OS maps as Crag Hill but formerly Eel Crag, this name is now given on maps to the northern face of the fell. Confused? Well this happens a lot hereabouts. Anyway, the views of the mountain and from the mountain are excellent. The craggy face is so well defined and the summit panorama takes in all the major Lakeland fells. Many ascents taken here are done as part of the Grasmoor to Causey Pike ridge walk which is really rather good, although as I have mentioned before sometimes on these trips you don't get to see the true character of a particular mountain as intimately as you would in a direct ascent. To see the best of Eel Crag and Crag Hill approach from the eastern paths for a real eye full!

Centre of substance, of all natural things,
These exciting heights cheerfully sing,
In midst of fellows, friends, lofty peers,
Clear paths on here most commandingly steer.

Along the ridges the narrow-necked crests,
Up from valleys, seamed gullies ahead,
Summoning Sail Pass or Coledale Hause,
Eel Crag often used open side doors.

On top of the world unveils vast scene,
Mountains and mountains in sunlight they gleam,
Swirl How to Scafell, Pillar to Red Pike,
Displaying powerful strength in momentous might.

ESK PIKE

Region: South **Height:** 2,904 ft **Grid Ref:** NY236074

I like Esk Pike because it's a hard-working mountain shouldering the many crossing paths in its upper and lower hause. Now not many walkers will set out with this mountain as their main aim but it is likely if you are heading for Bowfell or especially Scafell way you will set foot on its slopes and this fell is always fondly remembered. And those actually clambering over the craggy outcrops on its summit will be rewarded with excellent views all round. In mist the many paths can be confusing and some report that in the Ore Gap region compasses do not work correctly due to the heavy haematite deposits. But this is possibly one of those climbers' myths you hear from time to time.

A mountain in servitude to neighbours proud,
The fell walker fraternity praises it loud,
Esk Pike and its justly famous hause,
The road to adventures but worthy of pause.

Fast winds sweep the high pass,
Whether fair or foul the forecast,
Many paths here that attend the dales,
Many footsteps fall en route to vale.

Panoramic summit view a Scafell delight,
Awesome on heavenly clear starry night,
Or a rest break and picnic during the day,
As the mountain you find is often half way.

FAIRFIELD

Region: East **Height:** 2,864 ft **Grid Ref:** NY358117

The Fairfield Horseshoe is quite rightly a famous walk on this mountain's southern flanks, taking several other heights in along the way. This side of the mountain is a vast green valley and is totally passive, a big difference to the rocky northern side where bare sharp crags rise out of the long valley of Deepdale. The way from Deepdale is an interesting and more challenging variation along with that from Dovedale with many ways that lead to the summit. Here there is a rough stony plateau and the views are good of all the major fells and taking in Windermere and Coniston lakes. As always, take care here in mist. The top is confusing despite many cairns, and danger lies close to the north and west in the form of sudden precipices.

This mountain stands tall in Lakeland dreams,
With famous route encompassed in vista,
The subject of many pictorial postcard scene,
Brought from the shops by the humble visitor.

Here the southern broad back of Fairfield,
Shows its pleasant passive green hide,
To those many thronging to horseshoe,
On paths from Grasmere to Ambleside.

With the north approach complete contrast,
For grass gives way to rocky violent vale,
Desolate valley climbs to sudden steep crags
The intimate secrets of dark shaded Dovedale.

FELLBARROW

Region: West **Height:** 1,365 ft **Grid Ref:** NY132243

A gentle hill near Loweswater best climbed from Low Lorton village. Not the most popular of walks but little can be said against it with the mindful solitude that can be gained here, typical of the heights on the edge of Lakeland proper, and your only likely company being the fence running over the hill. No lakes or tarns can be seen here but the height-restricted view is diverse otherwise, especially towards the northern mountains and the western sea.

**Rolling hills, gentle breeze,
Pleasant pastures, panorama tease,
Rolling hills, run free,
Solway Firth, Irish Sea.
Rolling hills, brothers we,
Standing still, mountains see.**

FLEETWITH PIKE

Region: West Height: 2,126 ft Grid Ref: NY205141

A well-known height especially when seen from Buttermere and Honister Pass with quite an imposing outline on view. This fell is often a starting or finishing point for walks to Haystacks, Grey Knotts or the further adventure of Great Gable. You can actually enter the mountain here at the working mining museum which is situated at the top of the pass (giving you a 1,100-foot head start).Although you can continue onto the summit from the car park, the pike itself is certainly best climbed from the farm at its foot. The view from the summit back down the valley towards the lake is one of the many highlights of this region with the water's reflections so special on a calm day.

To see the world's best green slate divine,
Visit the working museum of Honister Mine,
Enter the mountain, see its heart,
Learn of old miners, their historical part.

Then climb to climax from Gatesgarth Farm,
Crucifix on crag should not alarm,
For there is a monument on Low Raven,
Fanny Mercer's memorial, white cross haven.

Fleetwith Edge challenges now in four stages,
Last one might have you laughing for ages,
For it fools you, thinking it's the final height,
But there's still a way to go to summit spike.

View is astounding, a fine prospect,
Great Gable and Pillar unveiled aspect,
Down towards lake, Oh Buttermere valley,
The sight of which makes spirits rally.

FROSWICK

Region: Far East Height: 2,362 ft Grid Ref: NY435085

Froswick is one of those fells that is a means to an end, used en route to more rewarding heights. The one really interesting eye-catching feature, but also a curse to the foot, is the ravine of Blue Gill, where the scree gully drops dramatically down from the summit. The top is small and lacking good views, although Langdale and Scafell can be seen along with the impressive summit cairns of neighbours. Best climbed from Troutbeck in the main as the Kentmere side of the fell is relatively pathless.

Not a grand place to head in a hurry,
Unless you're a fan of Blue Gill scree gully,
Dropping from summit to valley below,
Millions of rocks to stub your toe,
The best view it hasn't but ridge link is fine,
Thornthwaite and Ill Bell more worth your time.

GAVEL FELL

Region: North West Height: 1,726 ft Grid Ref: NY117184

Gavel Fell is at the centre of the heights around Loweswater. The south-west ridge, which runs to the top, is damp to say the least. Blake Fell stands in the way of the good seaward view but the sights toward Grasmoor have merit and make the wet ascent worthwhile. A couple of tarns, High Nook and Floutern, can be found hereabouts, lying to the northern and southern boundaries respectively.

This un-shapely mount does not inspire,
Wet marshy ground adds fuel to the fire
But anywhere in Lakeland it's better to be,
Than stuck in an office indeterminately,
So soggy boots are worth the prize,
For wholesome fresh air and a view that's nice.

GIBSON KNOTT

Region: Central **Height:** 1,385 ft **Grid Ref:** NY319099

Gibson Knott is a low ridge often travelled along as part of the Greenburn circuit taking in the more famous Helm Crag. The summit height here is often disputed, as when you are amongst the rocky knolls it's hard to tell the highest point. Sometimes the western knoll is marked by a cairn laying its claim to the prize. Being central the all-round view is not a bad one but because of the low height gained not as expansive as you may have hoped.

> **Greenburn bottom graded,**
> **Arise Gibson Knott,**
> **Adorned fringed crest.**
>
> **Steep flanks serrated,**
> **Humps, lumps, bumps,**
> **Middle rocky ridge.**

GLARAMARA

Region: South **Height:** 2,569 ft **Grid Ref:** NY246104

Glaramara is an impressive part of a long ridge that runs all the way to Esk Hause, a very important mountain pass in this region. The slightly unusual mouthful of a name means in Norse, "Hill with the mountain hut by a chasm". The hanging valley of Combe Gill adds value to walks along its northern heights and the many subsidiary tops, along with additional small tarns, make this a worthy adventure. The views from the summit heights are excellent, especially towards the Skiddaw range. Walks from here can be extended if you're sturdy of leg with Bowfell and the Scafells the target of many camping valley hoppers.

Towering twin peaks rise from verdant cloth of grass,
This is Glaramara, magnitude midst of Borrowdale,
A mountain of glacial green grace in ancient standing,
Whose northerly perspective panorama opens grand,
Where one may halt, meditate true nature's inspiration,
The loving eternal flow of beauty's infinite land.

GLENRIDDING DODD

Region: East **Height:** 1,450 ft **Grid Ref:** NY381175

Glenridding Dodd is one of those small character heights with a good view and can be climbed from its namesake village or from the water's edge at Stybarrow Crag. Ascents will often continue onto Sheffield Pike. Nearby also is the old Greenside Mine which in Victorian times yielded lead and silver leading to the growth of the village here. Mineral wealth has been firmly replaced by tourism and Glenridding village is a favourite stopping point for many adventurers Helvellyn or Ullswater ferry-bound.

Honour and glory is not always found,
On highest point far from the ground,
There's joy in Lakeland's smaller heights,
For this one serves Ullswater sights,
Look down the lake from up above,
Take in the beauty, pure natural love.

GOWBARROW FELL

Region: East **Height:** 1,578 ft **Grid Ref:** NY408219

Gowbarrow Fell doesn't look very photogenic but found on its lower slopes is one of the most visited features in the Lake District, but more on that in the poem. This feature is not the fell's only claim to fame, as Dorothy Wordsworth recorded in her 1802 journal about a walk in Gowbarrow Park where she saw many daffodils by the waterside. William Wordsworth read this journal in 1804 and hence one of the world's most famous poems was born.

Gowbarrow is a very famous fell,
The people flock here when the waters swell....
*"But hang on mate, don't go so fast!
That name's not famous, what's the fuss?"*

Well if you let me finish my verse now,
I will tell you of a place that will make you go wow!
So please let this poem go full course,
For this ditty is all about Aira Force.

Two stone bridges cross the watery drop,
Where many a photographer duly stop,
Two hundred foot, freely flowing fast falls,
Creating deep sounds and misty wall.

The grandstand feature is one of the best
And easy to walk to, not much of a test,
Many will start from Park Brow Foot,
Returning to tearoom in roundabout route.

GRANGE FELL

Region: Central **Height:** 1,362 ft **Grid Ref:** NY264162

Although Grange Fell is a small height easily gained from the nearby villages of Rosthwaite and Grange itself, this mountain has a lot of character, loved by locals and tourists alike, especially for the excellent viewpoint from the summit of King's How. The land here was one of the first purchases of the National Trust back in 1910, the money mainly coming from public subscription at the bequest of the then President, Princess Louise, sister of King Edward VII. A beautifully worded slate plaque on the summit commemorates how the fell was dedicated to the King. Near the foot of the fell is the famous large boulder, the Bowder Stone.

Rising from forest of birch, Lakeland utopia unfolds,
Richly adorned in graceful glades of golden green,
A crown of crags encircles this oasis of beauty,
Lush foliage sweeps from Bowder Stone base,
To the high heather pinnacle head of King's How,
Where the elevations rise and fall across plateau,
Like windswept waves on Derwentwater flow.

GRASMOOR

Region: North West **Height:** 2,795 ft **Grid Ref:** NY174203

Next to Crummock Water the steep-sided flank of the high peak of Grasmoor is unmistakable, its western side rising dramatically to the summit from where the view is excellent. The east–west ridge runs along the rest of the Grasmoor range taking in amongst others Crag Hill, Scar Crags, Sail and Causey Pike. Fun direct ascents can be taken from the lake but be warned, this involves climbing 2000 feet in about half a mile. Coledale Hause to the east can be used to gain the main hub of the range and this adventure opens up many possibilities to ridge walkers. Unlike a lot of the Lake District fells this mountain has no recorded history of mining.

Stern the face on high northern throne,
The busted crags, the rocky ribbed bones,
Sheer and sudden rises monolith altar,
Guarding from dark tower fair Crummock Water.

Bracken hollows, spurs of fine heather,
Grasmoor End falls down into nethers,
Dove Crag defends the edge on the tether,
Tipping its sides into vast amphitheatre.

GRAY CRAG

Region: Far East **Height:** 2,293 ft **Grid Ref:** NY227117

Gray Crag is a grassy ridge that runs off the parent fell of Thornthwaite Crag. On its shoulder Hayeswater is nestled and at its foot is the village of Hartsop. Ascents are often taken along the well-worn path that leads to the water's edge and then heads up the steep flanks to the summit itself which has an excellent view of the Helvellyn range. Alternatively also go to the opposing edges of the summit platform for great views down the valleys. Threshthwaite Mouth and then Pasture Beck make for a good alternative to ascent or descent on a Lakeland walk that will not disappoint.

From Pasture Beck to high Hayeswater,
Steep-sided flanks do not falter,
Drama rising like a God with thunder,
Deep gullies sharply split asunder,
Spiralling views from plateau atop,
Striking down valley, village of Hartsop.

GRAYSTONES

Region: North West **Height:** 1,496 ft **Grid Ref:** NY177266

Deep within the woods of the Darling How Plantation is a lovely waterfall and in truth this is the real highlight of Graystones. The rest of this small fell is a gentle grassy slope all round and makes for a pleasant easy walk. The Whinlatter Pass road runs round its foot and a quick ascent can be made from Scawgill Bridge. The summit is grass and the view is a little bland by Lakeland standards but saying that, still worthy.

Whinlatter winds round,
Sloping gentle ground,
Lorton valley scene,
Quiet, pleasant, serene,
Fine the waterfall,
Spout Force calls.

GREAT BORNE

Region: West **Height:** 2,021 ft **Grid Ref:** NY124163

Seen from Ennerdale this fell has a striking appearance and is often climbed from the car park at the base of Bowness Knott, a low subsidiary of Great Borne. Ascents from Buttermere via Floutern Pass were once very popular but the ground has now become very boggy. The fell has a good view, especially of the Loweswater fells. Locals refer to this mountain as Herdus.

**Riding high in dark western skies,
The windswept clouds they fast fly by.....**

**Solitary Great Borne,
Busy paths now long forlorn,
From Ennerdale your profile towers,
Buttress ridge your strength and power.**

GREAT CALVA

Region: North **Height:** 2,264 ft **Grid Ref:** NY291312

Great Calva sits at the head of a geological fault running through the heart of the Lakes and as a consequence you can view all the way south to Thirlmere and beyond. The view north sadly disappoints due to nearby fells blocking the vista. The pyramid-shaped fell, like several in the the plain of the Skiddaw Forest region (unusual name as there are no trees), is heathery and can be very wet underfoot with hard rock only making the occasional show. The sheepfolds in these parts are not your usual Lakeland type so often catch the walker's eye and camera. On the low ground the River Caldew begins to form with rain from the slopes of Skiddaw and very quickly grows in strength.

**Pyramid tower that stands so fair,
High over plain with heather-scented airs
And the Caldew exuberant in youthful vigour,
Flows with purpose the burgeoning river,
Here see the sheepfolds alone unique,
Circular in shape, art work complete.**

GREAT CARRS

Region: South Height: 2,585 ft Grid Ref: NY271009

Great Carrs is part of the end of a long ridge that runs down from Swirl How which is the high end of the Coniston range. Most people will climb this fell from a marked path off the Wrynose Pass road or from Little Langdale via Wet Side Edge. I prefer the former as it's interesting to watch the cars struggle up this famous road at 5 mph. After leaving the road there is a surprise in store as you climb the slope to the summit, for here the mountainside suddenly drops away opening up Greenburn and with some excellent views. Nearby on the slope of Broad Slack the sad remains of a crashed WW2 Canadian Air Force Halifax bomber can be found along with a memorial.

Three Shire Stone marks the path laid,
Up mountain moulded as curved scythe blade,
Great Carrs gentle grade of summit slope surprises,
For its eastern delights have many devices,
The profound perch on grand lofty precipice
Falls abruptly to the airy Greenburn abyss.

GREAT COCKUP

Region: North Height: 1,726 ft Grid Ref: NY273333

Great Cockup really doesn't have much going for it in all honesty unless you're summit bagging or shooting grouse. The view of Skiddaw from its heights is certainly the highlight although at most times of the year you will have to fight through bracken to get there. The name has obvious connotations but sexual it is not, Cock Up in old English (cocc hop) meaning secluded valley. If you haven't been to this fell I make no excuses for the short poem here.

Some may laugh at the suspect name,
Who am I to curse and blame,
The bracken jungle fell I won't belittle,
It could be worse, it could be little!

GREAT CRAG

Region: Central **Height:** 1,444 ft **Grid Ref:** NY269147

The heights of the northern fells of the Central Region are often boggy moorland plateaus. Great Crag is a rare exception having a prominent rocky top. The steep-sided fell, when approached from Rosthwaite in Borrowdale, (as described in the poem), provides a really interesting and beautiful walk, especially if including the popular path to Dock Tarn. Although the summit view is a little restricted it is still good when viewing Borrowdale and the mountains behind.

Lose yourself in luxuriant labyrinth,
Weave round verdant hill and hummock,
Skirting saturated swamps,
Skipping random stepping stones,
Over the free-flowing gills,
Passing wooded slopes.

Till your footfall rises,
A pilgrim on grey rocky path,
You find yourself drawn in,
A part of nature's dream,
Arriving at pinnacle in peace,
Spirit on the wind.

GREAT DODD

Region: East **Height:** 2,812 ft **Grid Ref:** NY342205

Great Dodd certainly lives up to its name with its rounded profile and wide tract of land. The fell runs off from the northern end of the Helevellyn range at an acute angle and runs downhill for five miles to Troutbeck. Ascents from most directions can be a little wet under foot and there are not many marked paths. I found attacking the gentle slopes from Legburthwaite in the west to be the best option. The view is a good one from the summit with glimpses of most of Lakeland in sight and on a clear day the Northern Pennines can be seen.

Simple subtle standing,
Gentle gradients gliding,
Extensive sprawling slopes,
Verdant, windswept, wilderness,
Allotted nature's blessing,
Appointed Great Dodd.

GREAT END

Region: South **Height:** 2,968 ft **Grid Ref:** NY226084

Great End on the northern point of the Scafell range certainly lives up to its name. The fell is not just popular with walkers but mountain climbers too and is a place where you often find wild campers. The craggy face is dark and imposing, and riven by some deep gullies – you're in real mountain country here. Ascended from the valleys of Borrowdale, Eskdale, Wasdale and Langdale, the fell itself lies on the cusp of the major crossroads of the ever popular Esk Hause. Some walkers en route to Scafell miss out by not visiting this mountain and to explore its heights is highly recommended. The summit view is most excellent in every regard, especially from the north-western cliff face where the Borrowdale vista breathtakingly unfolds.

No delusions of grandeur for Great End,

No lie in the name for this domed mass,

This anchor for the Scafell high plateau,

Showing its ugly broad massive strength,

In Gothic buttress forever in shadow,

Grim and harsh the stark scene here,

Where ravens soar on unseen winds,

High above dangerous dark deadly seams,

Of rock strewn waste and fierce wilderness,

Only mellowed by range of perspective,

Abundantly delivered by views reflected.

GREAT GABLE

Region: West Height: 2,949 ft Grid Ref: NY211104

Great Gable, lying in the heart of the Western region, is an undoubted gem in the crown of Lakeland and very deserving of the title "Great". The fell can be approached from many directions, all of them a fulfilling adventure and every single one has merit. You must climb this mountain on a clear day for the summit provides one of the best views in the Lake District, if not the best. The walk round the Gable Girdle, a complete circuit mainly at about mid height, is also a very popular route. English rock climbing has its historic roots here on this mountain beginning in Victorian times.

Enter legend and mountain fable,
Time to climb august Great Gable
For you must prove your sturdy worth,
Walking on stalwart hallowed earth.

High in the sky scene pervades profound,
Desert of stones depth all around,
Falling in places called Hell's Gate,
Where rock strikes out at bold Great Napes.

Now if you go traversing the Gable Girdle,
Many problems you'll have to try and hurdle,
Those many ups and downs will not be forgot,
From Windy Gap to high Kern Knotts.

Conquering this climax many truly aspire,
To battle onwards, upwards stoic, never tire,
And fight the fears of unknown extremes,
Ascending heights with joys set supreme.

The sights to see the eyes cannot hold,
Far summits many, land and sea unfolds,
The best view they say that does not fail,
Heads down to Wastwater and fairest Wasdale.

GREAT MELL FELL

Region: East **Height:** 1,762 ft **Grid Ref:** NY397254

Great Mell Fell is often seen on the main road from Penrith to Keswick and is an outlier of the Helvellyn Range, looking like a pair of breasts or upturned pudding moulds when seen with its twin sister, Little Mell Fell! The marshland surrounding this area can be a bit stark but once the paths uphill are found this turns into a pleasant low-level walk. Remains of an MOD rifle range can be found hereabouts. On the summit are several deformed windswept larches and a Bronze Age burial mound. You'll find the view is excellent as the fell stands in virtual glorious isolation away from the neighbouring mountains.

A pudding bowl mount the greater twin,
Marker, portal, to Helvellyn begin,
Standing aloof away from the crowd,
Where guns were once heard firing aloud.

Standing in marshland desolate and grim,
Your rifles silenced, no longer a din,
Eastern slopes a fertile, colourful wood,
Summit trees, winds grotesquely withstood.

GREAT RIGG

Region: East **Height:** 2,513 ft **Grid Ref:** NY355104

Part of the famous Fairfield Horseshoe walk, Great Rigg is an easy sloping ridge running to the heights. Many will start out from Ambleside on this 10-mile (round about) walk, taking in some stunning views, including those from the summit. Many a lake and tarn can be seen from here and this more than makes up for the relative dullness of the mountain. On a clear day up to ten different large waters can be seen.

A gentle giant can be found,
On way to Fairfield Horseshoe round,
Easing up softly on grass slopes shoulder,
Above Tongue Gill there's rock and boulder,
Great Rigg summit is quite a bland place,
Though vista's grand for viewing lakes.

GREAT SCA FELL

Region: North **Height:** 2,136 ft **Grid Ref:** NY291338

The Uldale fells are a pleasant green land with little rock, making for good pastures, so you're more likely to meet sheep than another walker for many miles in this region. This fell has two summits, Little Sca Fell and Great Sca Fell, and they can be approached from the minor road that skirts round by Orthwaite. The summit view is excellent in the direction of the Solway Firth and Scottish border, but the mass of Skiddaw blocks the main view of Lakeland, although a distant view of Bowfell can be seen on the clearest of days.

Verdant valleys surround,
Northern height ground
Three ridges raise,
Merging meeting grazed,
Sheep pastures grow,
Flocked sheep flow.

GREEN CRAG

Region: South **Height:** 1,604 ft **Grid Ref:** SD200982

Green Crag is one of those small fells in Lakeland rich in beauty and character. This fell was mined for iron, and peat was also extracted here. An old sled gate route leads up from Eskdale to the craggy summit where a little bit of fun scrambling on rock is required to reach the top. The view is good of the Southern fells and there is also a glimpse of the sea.

Path from Woolpack Inn serene,
Dreamy picture postcard scene,
Heavy cloak of pleasant heather,
Joy beheld in summer's weather.

Head along the old peat roads,
Rise to Green Crag's serrated edge,
Scafell, Bowfell call from distance,
Your heart to mountains you will pledge.

GREEN GABLE

Region: West **Height:** 2,628 ft **Grid Ref:** NY214107

Green Gable is seen lying on the side of Great Gable showing this fell's place in the grander scheme of things, a sloping bridge to the greater prize. If the mountain but stood alone it would be famous in its own right with a respectable height and great views. However, it is dominated by its near neighbour, as all eyes and legs strain towards the master. Only the lower slopes of this fell are green, with the summit a desert of rock and stone. Windy Gap is the famous adjoining pass that sits on the shoulder of both fells.

Hurry! Hurry! Hurry!
To greater Gable,
The masses scurry,
Not stopping surveying,
Gable Crag displaying.

Used! Used! Used!
Grand height stands,
Stepping stone abused,
Suppliant subservient fell,
Serving master well.

GREY CRAG

Region: Far East **Height:** 2,093 ft **Grid Ref:** NY497072

I found Grey Crag a lonely solitary place mainly because it lies on the fringes of Lakeland proper and when climbed from the A6 Shap Road you're not likely to meet a fellow walker either up or down. The route is not the most exciting, and it can be very wet. But the rocky short ridge summit has merit as the viewpoint is expansive, especially east to the Pennines and west to the Scafell and Coniston range of mountains.

High link to the Pennines,
Wet moor turns to rock and crag,
As peat gives way to stony stock heart.
Panoramic the pace, seen in wide sweeping place,
Silent, solitary, here lonely paths prevail,
Not a place to wander in mist, rain or hail.

GREY FRIAR

Region: South **Height:** 2,526 ft **Grid Ref:** NY259003

A large part of the eastern wall of the Duddon valley is made up of Grey Friar and although belonging to the Coniston Fells all water falls off its slopes in this direction. The mountain was once mined for copper although not as vastly or as profitably as elsewhere on this range. Despite its size it is rarely climbed for the fell lacks the interesting characteristics of its counterparts. It does, however, lay claim to the best view of Scafell from its summit.

The hermit Grey Friar stands aloof,
Not many a guest will he receive,
For lacking in feature is his doom,
A silent watcher prevailing he perceives.

He has a secret I will tell you,
Swear in blood it won't be told!
For the green grassy domed summit,
Has a marvel you must behold.

As the bulky bland mountain,
Only popular amongst the few,
Has the best seat to praise the King,
Magnificent unrivalled westward view.

GREY KNOTTS

Region: West **Height:** 2,287 ft **Grid Ref:** NY217125

A fell with a lot of character and history, and being near the heart of Borrowdale very popular amongst walkers. Climbers too love this place as Gillercomb Buttress, on the map as Raven Crag, provides a challenge, and the area is littered with large rocks suitable for beginners' bouldering. An old plumbago (graphite) mine can be found on the end of Newhouse Gill that dates back to the 16th century and eventually provided material for the later Keswick pencil industry. What's left of the ancient trees, the Borrowdale Yews, can also be seen on its slopes. The summit view is very good, especially of the Buttermere valley and the Scafell massif.

Here on the slopes there's much to find,
Cascading falls, abandoned mines,
The rocky towers, turrets, tor,
Tarns sprinkled random on crown floor,
Where giant prospect comes to view,
With Buttermere scene of beauty true.

GRIKE

Region: West **Height:** 1,601 ft **Grid Ref:** NY086141

Grike is one of those Western hills whose slopes drop gently down towards the sea. Part of the Lank Rigg group, this fell is locally known by the name of the huge cairn seen on its summit and is best climbed from Ennerdale Bridge up past the gill waterfalls or from Kinniside Stone Circle. There are good views of the sea and Western fells from the summit, but Crag Fell obscures the rest of the panorama. A failed iron mine was worked here on its lower slopes in Victorian times.

Fine waterfalls can be seen,
On walk up to Ben Gill ravine,
Weather reports for the nation,
Taken daily from summit station,
Here the view seaward spans,
Grand cairn here called Stone Man.

GRISEDALE PIKE

Region: North West **Height:** 2,595 ft **Grid Ref:** NY198225

In this poem I describe the path taken from the village of Braithwaite up to the heights of Grisedale Pike, a well-used and fun ascent. The mountain is situated in a very strategic place, especially with its pass of Coledale Hause feeding the rest of the main mountain ridge with routes going in many directions. The views from the summit are extensive on the clearest of days with not just Lakeland in sight; the Cheviots, the Pennines and even the mountains in Ireland over a hundred miles away can be seen! I liked this fell as it had a steely character in places, being well used, and undoubtedly abused, by the hand of man, with mining, forestry and recreation having taken their toll. It is also one of those mountains where the wind seems to really blow hard, even on a fine day.

From Braithwaite a popular undertaking,
As Grisedale Pike so fun in the making,
Rising to ridges Sleet How and Kinn
The last stage to summit, arête tiring,
Here the winds in strength really expose,
So checkout the view and onwards proposed,
For we still have hopefully, plenty of time,
Heading to Coledale Hause for Force Crag Mine,
Two cascades fall fast, flowing from tip.
Footpath past mine road, the returning trip.

HALLIN FELL

Region: Far East Height: 1,273 ft Grid Ref: NY433198

One of an elite band of small Lakeland fells that is a real charm and with a perfect location being surrounded on three sides by Ullswater. The grandstand view does not stop at the lake though, with mountains behind in the Martindale valley system putting on a good show. A great way to visit is via the Ullswater ferry to Howtown where the ascent is short to the summit cairn. Combine this with a return path along the lakeside path to Patterdale and you will have had one of your most memorable days.

Rich rewards duly await,
Hallin Fell unrivalled viewscape,
Obelisk stands, summit marked,
Gentle smooth, joyful lark,
Modest effort, grand the prize,
Martindale exuberant, Ullswater thrives.

HARD KNOTT

Region: South **Height:** 1,801 ft **Grid Ref:** NY231023

If you are in your car driving up and down the famous road pass of Hard Knott it really would be rude not to stop at the top and continue on foot to the summit. After all, most of the hard work has been done for you! The fell holds no secrets but has many charms with the view from the top truly excellent, especially of Scafell and the Eskdale valley. On its lower slopes and near to the road can be found the Roman fort, which is well worth a visit. But a warning to day trippers stepping out of the car with nice shoes on; the very short climb to the walls can be wet and boggy.

Follow the contour of spiralling contortions,
The winding, tricky, twisting narrow road,
Here lies Hard Knott of ancient famous name,
Of many delights a plentiful treasure load.

The summit height unpretentious craggy top,
Place of renown, respected visions gift,
Seen in magnificence, glorious Eskdale head,
Classical performance nature's melodic lift.

Below castle fort defies the weathering years,
Ghostly vapours stand guard on misty earth,
Over centuries these sentries keep watch,
For under Roman yoke Brigantia bled its worth.

HARRISON STICKLE

Region: Central Height: 2,415 ft Grid Ref: NY281074

I chose Harrison Stickle to be the cover photo on this book for many reasons, not least because it's one of my favourites but also it is the eye-catching view often seen by those folk travelling on the Windermere steamers and boats from Ambleside or those travelling along the road to Langdale. The panorama often stops people in their tracks to gaze in wonder and awe, inspiring them on to the heights above. They will not be disappointed; the view from the mountain is as good as or better than the view of it. The paths up the ever so popular Stickle Ghyll and the more adventurous scrabble up the water course of Dungeon Ghyll (not for the inexperienced) really make this a mountain to return to – keep an eye out for me!

Wandering along shores of Low Wood, Windermere,
My eye is drawn to familiar friend on far horizon,
Ah, that famous silhouette of hallowed heights,
Glorified in full grandeur by setting sun.
The towering peaks stand in shadow – Lord of Langdale.

My mind floods with marvellous memories,
Oh those cherished days in all weathers tested,
That have seared into my very heart and soul,
Becoming part of my very being, my essence,
Time after time till man became mountain.

Water flows like blood coursing in rugged ravines,
The deep dark chasm drama of Dungeon Ghyll,
Intimacy! Shocking intimacy showing mountain bones,
Ravages bared by waters raging measure,
Mellowed here and there by mother's kinder hand.

From ghyll to pinnacle on reminiscent wing,
I look down on world far, far below,
Free from the pressures of modern life,
I sit on clouds contemplating, meditating,
The dynamic dualism a pole's reversed mirror.

HART CRAG

Region: East Height: 2,697 ft Grid Ref: NY368113

Hart Crag is a south-eastern ridge that runs down off Fairfield and as a consequence is often climbed as part of the famous horseshoe route. The most interesting features of this fell itself, however, are not seen to good advantage on this route and the best way for me and other crag hunters is via the valley of Deepdale, heading up to the impressive sights of Link Cove. Here you will get very intimate with the rock in this most desolate wild mountain region, so take care to follow the path to the heights. The summit view is somewhat restricted by Dove Crag and Fairfield but the valleys below put on a good show, as does the view west with the grand Scafells.

Rising from demolished Deepdale,
Where the devastation's truly great,
Whether there is any path up beck,
Is really open to quizzical debate.

More than a stepping stone,
To Fairfield's grand heights,
Hart Crag is grim, rugged,
South face a fearsome fright!

Black and Earnest Crag
Defend the roughest peak,
Link Cove grandly guards,
Wild hollow not for the weak.

HART SIDE

Region: East **Height:** 2,480 ft **Grid Ref:** NY359198

After reading a lot of the guidebooks and then visiting this fell I think Hart Side is often done an injustice. Yes, the view from the summit is curtailed because of its width, location and the Helvellyn range being close, but the distant viewscape of mountain horizons is 360 degrees all round. This fell is mostly gently sloping grass with some occasional rock outcrops which feed the random cairns placed here and there. An excellent view of Ullswater can be seen on the mountain's lower slopes called the Brown Hills and the fell is best climbed from this direction.

Best visited along the lakeside flank,
The summit view doesn't greatly rank,
From lower Brown Hills you can see best,
Ullswater charms put your eyes to test,
Take your picture from old stone wall,
Water surrounded by mountains tall.

HARTER FELL (ESKDALE)

Region: South **Height:** 2.129 ft **Grid Ref:** SD218997

When seen from Eskdale, Harter Fell certainly has a lot of charm, as does the whole beautiful valley in which it resides. Nature has painted some of its best pictures here with that lovely combination of rugged rock and rich foliage. The view from the summit tors (grand to scramble on) is excellent seawards and nearby the Scafell range and Bowfell put on a grand show. The other added attraction for some of us old campaigners is the well-deserved pint at the nearby Woolpack Inn.

Ascending swiftly from wooded grove and dell,
Through thick foliage, flora-laden heath,
Spring grey turrets of grace atop Harter Fell,
Eskdale lauded loveliness displays beneath.

Richly rewarded those climbing highest degree,
The exulted wide expanse of pyramidical heights,
More colours in a rainbow you never did see,
Overwhelming, irresistible, Mother Earthly delights.

HARTER FELL (MARDALE)

Region: Far East **Height:** 2,552 ft **Grid Ref:** NY549093

This poem describes the main old zigzag trade routes up from Haweswater and over the summit of Harter Fell, now very popular paths for walkers. The view from the summit is good and if you go carefully to the edge of the crags nearby, a great view of the lake can be seen.

There's a thoroughly enjoyable roundabout route,
At end of Haweswater warm up your boots,
Head up Gatescarth Beck and zigzag to pass,
Following the groove of shepherds' past graft,
Graceful curve to summit, rounding the crags,
Stand and face lake you won't feel aghast,
Then head off to Nan Bield, a treat in store,
Ridge down crag to Small Water shores,
Here is beauty, ranked high in a tarn,
Path down beck and you return unharmed.

HARTSOP ABOVE HOW

Region: East **Height:** 1,923 ft **Grid Ref:** NY383120

Hartsop above How is part of the north-east ridge of Hart Crag and runs down from here to Low Wood dropping to Brothers Water. In these woods can be found the remains of the Hartsop Hall lead mine. The trees here are a very rare example of native woodland. Locally the fell is sometimes referred to as Gill Crag, the summit of which is a series of grassy rocky knolls with good close up views of the valleys either side.

Sheathed in well-wooded end,
Where still Brothers Water tend,
Sharp curved blade, the ridge rising,
Steep grey Dovedale Slabs surprising,
Here then on Gill Crag you stand,
Admiring the beloved beauty grand.

HARTSOP DODD

Region: Far East **Height:** 2,028 ft **Grid Ref:** NY412118

When seen from its namesake village, Hartsop Dodd gives the impression of being an impressive independent fell, but it is in fact one of the ridges running off Caudale Moor. Ascents are often made from the village or from many of the paths leading up its western side. The summit is crossed by an old stone wall and a timber post marks the highest point. The view is excellent of the local fells and the beautiful valley of Dovedale is shown to really good effect.

Wood and water,
Stock and stone,
Rising so arresting,
North ridge dome,
Here the eye,
Will easily roam,
To Dovedale heart,
Welcome Patterdale home.

HAYCOCK

Region: West **Height:** 2,615 ft **Grid Ref:** NY144107

Haycock is a very remote fell and as a consequence is not often climbed. This is a shame as this dome-shaped mountain has a lot of character, the best of which is its particularly fine profile view towards the Scafell range. If you move around the summit some of the waters come into view, Wastwater to the south especially. All mountains are windy by their nature. Some, such as this one, however, more so than others. Personally I love being exposed to a good hard strong wind; it all adds to the challenge of conquest!

Rugged remote,
Shouldered dome,
Moorland fringe,
Barren home.

Elements batter,
Summit stone,
Scafell range,
Vistas tone.

HAYSTACKS

Region: West **Height:** 1,959 ft **Grid Ref:** NY193131

There is no doubting that Haystacks has that special something despite being surrounded by grander heights. Its summit is full of interest with many surprises, and added to the fact that Alfred Wainwright wished his ashes to be placed here, then you can see why so many walkers now make a pilgrimage. It certainly is a favourite place of mine but not "the" favourite and my ashes are destined for a more accessible place, that for the moment I will keep secret (don't want to tempt fate seeing as I'm still living and breathing. But I suspect I may fall off of this place one day prompting the matter!). Anyway, the views here are excellent and they will catch your eye. But the real star here is the mountain itself.

In majestic midst of towering might,
Humble Haystacks flourishes in delights,
Discerning, discrete, not flaunting features,
Although proud the peaks, a subtle picture,
Hidden home to pools, tantalising tarns,
A true mountain Eden, a magical yarn,
Unassuming, arrayed in serpentine surprise,
This special soulful place full of spiritual highs,
The twisting, turning trails a medley of mystery,
A journey, adventure, your place down in history.

HELM CRAG

Region: Central **Height:** 1,329 ft **Grid Ref:** NY327094

It is no secret that Helm Crag is the day trippers' delight, being easily climbed from Grasmere village, the low height making it readily accessible. Newcomers to the Lakes can blood themselves here, the mountain being full of interest, especially in the form of the mountain outcrops, the most famous being the easily recognised Lion and the Lamb. The summit intrigue does not end here as the strange ridge formation looks almost man-made, although it is just one of those freaks of nature. The grand view looks to the Eastern fells nearby and towards Langdale and Coniston to the south-west.

Welcome to the Lion and the Lamb,
Its affectionate name across the land,
Walked easily from Grasmere way,
From valley to top in half the day.

The sides are steep and summit rough,
Great introduction to get mountain tough,
For no Lakeland tour is truly complete,
Without Helm Crag walked beneath your feet!

HELVELLYN

Region: East Height: 3,117 ft Grid Ref: NY342151

It's fair to say that my love affair with Helvellyn has remained strong and constant over the years. Many visitors will know why it is so, though some will leave the mountain in fear and trepidation after suffering vertigo on Striding Edge. The majority will go away with memories of a fabulous adventure on rocky ridges with stunning views all the way up and down. The western approach up bland grassy slopes does not compare even in the slightest to the eastern approaches and though many take this easier quick route to the heights they look on in awe from the summit watching those earning their rite of passage.

No greater or true honour have I found,
Than to walk on hallowed Helvellyn ground,
For held in my heart a woven legend lies,
When far from mountains, imagination does fly,
To this grand vision setting mind to heights,
Mystical manifestation of elemental delights.
All the delights I will personally name,
When climbing this bastion you'll be on your game,
Easily tackled from green-sloped west,
But please, I beg you, east is finest!
Patterdale, Glenridding are your humble start,
A full day's work ahead, be stout of heart.

The Hole in the Wall after Birkhouse Moor,
Is the beginning or end of Helvellyn grand door?
Look on in awe from Red Tarn paths,
Heights above, arms stretched out ready to grasp,
The right arm that grabs you is Swirral Edge
The left arm the famous long Striding Edge.
A steep rocky arête and celebrity crest,
Voted by footfall Lakeland's greatest,
Watch out for wind and snow-capped ice,
As a fall from here would be far from nice,
On the far end is an awkward slab,
If a friend's to hand they can help your grab.

Continued………..

Steep climb to summit past the Gough stone
For such a grand mountain there is no throne,
The top is bland and really quite pale,
As the earth is covered in broken shale,
There's a place to lunch in crossed walled slate,
Look out for sheep taking food off your plate!
The view surrounds and totally takes you in,
On a clear blue day you will certainly grin,
Mountains around North, East, South, West,
The panorama of the Scafells is for me the best,
In truth Helvellyn spoils you, found upon reflection,
Testament to devotees' great love and affection.

HEN COMB

Region: West **Height:** 1,670 ft **Grid Ref:** NY133181

Have I been a little harsh on Hen Comb in my poem? I don't think so. This really is a mountain fell for summit baggers only as it offers very little else, except the summit view being reasonable. The passage there though is often a boggy nightmare and I hereby challenge you to arrive at the summit with dry feet – picture evidence will be required!

To climb it once,
Is not nice.

To climb it twice,
Would be a vice.

To climb it thrice,
You must be mad.

To keep boots dry,
You would be glad!

To keep boots dry,
You would be glad!!

HERON PIKE

Region: East **Height:** 2.008 ft **Grid Ref:** NY305882

For most the ascent of Heron Pike is a primary stage of the Fairfield Horseshoe and although its grassy slopes are of little interest to the climber they do make a good place for a picnic with a good view of Windermere below. Walkers will set out from Rydal or Grasmere with the latter being the slightly better route as Alcock Tarn can be visited.

Another stepping stone,
On horseshoe path,
Or a half a day jolly,
With little graft.

The summit is grassy,
A quartz rock crown,
The smallness of top,
Gives rich views all around.

HIGH CRAG

Region: West **Height:** 2,441 ft **Grid Ref:** NY180140

High Crag sets a worthy challenge and the quest is to find the route safely to the summit when ascending from the popular environs of Buttermere. The route to the top is not at first obvious as dark deadly crags and steep scree slopes defend the front door. Hardy walkers include this fell in the popular High Stile ridge walk that also includes a visit to Red Pike. This area is rugged mountain country so as always, go suitably equipped.

Defences set strong and hard to reach,
Hot-blooded veins will seek the breach,
You should attack at Scarth Gap pass,
Any other attempts could be your last!
For only climbers go to Burtness Comb,
Without a rope here, you'll be entombed,
Mad fellows, fools, attempt the sea of scree,
Rock falls, slides, and grease slippery,
Rewards attained should you win through,
For your efforts alone have earned the view.

HIGH HARTSOP DODD

Region: East **Height:** 1,703 ft **Grid Ref:** NY393108

High Hartsop Dodd is often seen by those travelling by car over Kirkstone Pass. The fell is not often climbed in its own right, being a stepping stone to Little Hart Crag and Dove Crag. The only decent route is up the bold front of the fell which is steep and grassy, Kirkstonefoot being the starting point. The view from the summit is curtailed by higher fells nearby but this does not degrade its value with these seen in glorious detail, especially Dove Crag.

Dovedale elegance unfolds,
High Hartsop Dodd so brash, so bold,
So bold a front from valley floor,
So eye catching, profile adored,
Pyramid lines that so shapely rise,
From Brothers Water the heart doth cry.

HIGH PIKE (CALDBECK)

Region: North **Height:** 2,159 ft **Grid Ref:** NY318350

The saying "Caldbeck Fells are worth all England else" originates from this richly mined mineral region which created vast wealth. No less than twenty-three different ores have been mined here from the 16th century right up to 1966 when the last mine closed. The summit here has a lot of character too in the form of a large cairn, a wind shelter made from a ruined shepherd's hut and a slate memorial bench. A fire beacon also has been lit on the summit to mark occasional important events such as coronations and the millennium. The view of Lakeland is hidden behind the mass of Skiddaw but the vista seawards is good towards the Solway Firth. The true charm of the fell though is certainly its rich history.

Legendary mined mountain,
Olde England's hardcore worth,
Four hundred years of service,
Memories secreted under turf.

Watch for ancient levels,
Hidden by rock and heather parts,
Follow waters, especially Roughton Gill,
For evidence of industrial past.

HIGH PIKE (SCANDALE)

Region: East **Height:** 2,152 ft **Grid Ref:** NY373088

The path up High Pike leads from Ambleside and is often the secondary stage of the Fairfield Horseshoe. When viewed from High Sweden Bridge the fell gives the impression of being a remote peak with falling cliffs. This is a shame, as actually the hillside here is in fact part of the long southern ridge leading up to grander heights. The view ahead is obviously obscured by these but the view towards the town and Windermere itself is excellent.

Ambleside entrance
The horseshoe route,
Truly many tread this,
So well worn by boots.

From High Sweden Bridge
An old familiar sight,
The outline of Everest,
Though miniature in height!

The glints in the water,
Will catch your eye,
With view of the lake,
From grandstand on high.

HIGH RAISE (LANGDALE)

Region: Central **Height:** 2.500 ft **Grid Ref:** NY280095

High Raise is arguably at the very centre of the Lake District and despite this distinction it is not the most exciting of mountains with regard to its terrain. However, as a viewpoint this is entirely a different matter as its height and central location lead to superb views of all the major heights with the exception of the nearby Langdales, which look very much less flattering from behind! Further afield the Yorkshire Dales and Morecambe Bay put on a good show. The area around the summit has many paths and ridges leading out like spokes from a wheel hub.

At High White Stones
You enter
Panoramic paradise.
In all directions
Summits surround you
At centre.

Valleys radiate
Like spokes
On a wheel.
Which route to take,
What path
Is your fate?

HIGH RAISE (HIGH STREET)

Region: Far East **Height:** 2,631 ft **Grid Ref:** NY448135

The poem for High Raise takes on the fell from the slightly harder to reach western Haweswater approach and in my mind is far more interesting than the Martindale route. Before the main ascent there is a walk along the shoreline, with waterfalls and ancient ruins to investigate. The summit view westwards is very good with a very open panorama.

Steep side flank, Haweswater shore,
Whelter Bottom bracken floor,
Cross the beck at Waterfall Bridge,
Hunt for the ruins on South-East Ridge.

Then rise, rise, to scooped out hollow,
Path to Low Raise then you follow,
Lofty High Raise now grandly greet,
Follow road over top, Old High Street.

Harsh stony summit is quite the surprise,
Compared to neighbours' gentler grassy lies,
The view displayed, westward show on stand,
With vista presented, so glorious, so grand.

HIGH RIGG

Region: Central **Height:** 1,171 ft **Grid Ref:** NY308220

High Rigg is one of those lovely Sunday stroll types of fell, a true little gem, and is easily climbed with the reward of excellent views. People often remark that it resembles Lakeland in miniature, a kind of Lilliput model, and I would certainly go along with that assessment. I would also add that the vale as a whole has a very special feeling to it, hard to explain but it is almost as if the mountains are loving you.

A fell that stands alone,
Though has many visitors in the dale,
For church-marked path to High Rigg,
Starts at St John's in the Vale.
Not the hardest taxing climb you'll do,
It will render muscles little harm,
The heart will well at vista's view,
Presenting gorgeous graceful charm.

HIGH SEAT

Region: Central **Height:** 1,995 ft **Grid Ref:** NY287180

High Seat is undoubtedly an excellent viewpoint, the drawback being walking the wet peat bog summit heights that in truth are quite drab. The lower heights more than make up for this though being of far more interest and truly worthy of exploration.

Though pinnacle only worthy in respect of the view,
Grand lower slopes, adorned riches to pursue,
Coppice-lined crags in western waters wood,
Ashness Bridge and falls, delivering the goods,
Defined watersheds, sparkling beck, gill and tarn,
Streaming cascades displaying finest charms.

HIGH SPY

Region: North West **Height:** 2,142 ft **Grid Ref:** NY234162

We climb up High Spy in the poem from Grange in Borrowdale. This route has its drama in the challenge of the rake scramble and is also dramatic as the view is only slowly revealed as you ascend the final heights to the edge of the long crest. Following the fringe of crags here is great fun and this area is also loved by climbers as the quality of the volcanic rock is perfect for their pursuit. The view from the summit is good. Look out for an unnamed tarn further along towards the north top, where here the view opens up to Derwentwater.

High Spy with my little eye,
Something beginning with Grange,
Heading to path up Ellers Beck,
This ascent is well in range.

Reaching the barriers of rock ahead,
Make a beeline for High White Rake,
Breach in the wall is rugged and rough,
So care in the route you must take.

The length of Eel Crag comes into sight,
So exciting to boldly follow fringe face,
Arêtes, gullies, bold buttress cliffs,
Where climbers go to be put through their pace.

HIGH STILE

Region: West **Height:** 2,648 ft **Grid Ref:** NY170148

High Stile, the grandest mountain of the exciting Buttermere Three Route, is usually climbed as a traverse taking in Red Pike and High Crag but also can be tackled directly from the shores of the lake via the combs. The summit vista is excellent with the North Western fells putting on a cracking show with also Crummock Water and Ennerdale Water in view. A trip to the edge of the crags will bring Bleaberry Tarn into the panorama along with impressive dramatic crags and combs.

Long shadows thrown down on sylvan shores,
Born of the brooding menacing might,
The danger peril from the heights,
Deep the cuts of the serrated saw,
Upon the silver cloud canvas.

Piercing penetration smashing vales into ruination,
Gothic drama stands firm on fringed face,
The foreboding, forbidding fortress,
Defended buttress battlements,
Rock steady statement.

Dare you embark on this monumental mystery?
So substance straining, mind and body aching,
The twisting trials, beneath the rocky miles,
Zealous zenith, panorama pensive.
Not forlorn the faith, paths laid.

Well worth the prize....... hot dripping sweat sacrifice.

HIGH STREET

Region: Far East Height: 2,717 ft Grid Ref: NY440110

High Street, famous because it is named after the old Roman road that heads over its heights, really has a lot to offer other than its interesting history. The eastern climb up from Mardale at the end of Haweswater is one of the best ridge walks in the district with truly spectacular views all the way. This side of the mountain is mainly all craggy and at the foot of these can be seen the two tarns of Blea Water and Small Water. Blea Water attracts a lot of attention being in an immense corrie and is the deepest tarn in the Lake District at 200 feet. The summit is a flat plateau with an excellent view of the Pennines to the east and the mass of the Lake District mountains to the west, with the Helvellyn range particularly taking the eye.

Think of ancient soldiers, marauding bands,
Travelling high across this wild, windy land,
Now you the modern hiker cuts the classic path,
From Haweswater tree-tipped slope of grass,
Begin your ascent on prominent The Rigg,
This climb follows faithfully finger ridge,
Past Swine, Heron, Eagle, Rough Crag,
Steadily rising Blea Water left flank,
Caspel Gate rest, work Long Stile raise,
Then High Street summit, well done, let's praise.

HIGH TOVE

Region: Central **Height:** 1,690 ft **Grid Ref:** NY288166

High Tove is really just an upper marshland and outlier of High Seat with wet ascents whatever the weather from Watendlath on one side or Thirlmere on the other. The summit is very bland although if you like boggy depressions the Peewits is certainly for you, otherwise this is for summit baggers only. The views from the top are the only thing going for it really and these are good east and west. North and south though the panorama is blocked by neighbouring fells, the routes to which are swampy peat hags – my poem does not lie!

> Squelch.........squelch........squelch.
> If you like your boots dry,
> Then to High Tove do not fly.
>
> Squelch.........squelch........squelch.
> This wasteland summit so so wet,
> Take advice be in my debt.
>
> Squelch.........squelch........squelch.
> Even when there is a drought,
> Soggy feet are not in doubt.
> Squelch.........squelch........squelch.

HINDSCARTH

Region: North West **Height:** 2,385 ft **Grid Ref:** NY215165

Hindscarth is an interesting walk, especially beginning from the church at Newlands. From here you go over Scope End ridge to discover a real treat in the form of Goldscope Mine. The workings date from the 1560s when a very rich source of lead and copper was found here by imported German miners. It was so rich that they called it Gottesgab (God's gift). In all, about twenty minerals were mined here including the occasional pieces of gold and silver. The importance of this site to our heritage has now started to come to the attention of the authorities and hopefully its preservation will become a priority as the historical wealth here is as rich as the mine. The view from the summit is excellent, especially towards Skiddaw.

Have you the patience, have you the time,
To search the many spoil heaps and find
Precious metals from ancient mined depths,
Glistening gold and shining silver nuggets?

Now should your hunt not successfully succeed,
Stay away!! Keep Out!! Do not proceed!!
Down the oh so deep, dark, dangerous pan holes,
Or ghosts you will become, forgotten dead, lost souls.

Instead to the edge up Scope End you must raise,
The ridge way to the heights here you will praise,
As the easy summit comes without much drama
And with very pleasing picture panorama.

HOLME FELL

Region: South Height: 1,040 ft Grid Ref: NY315006

Holme Fell is rather dwarfed by the grander heights of the Coniston range. But looks can be deceptive and this is another of those little gems the Lake District throws up occasionally, and whilst it may be no Castle Crag, or Loughrigg for that matter, it is certainly worth mentioning in the same company. Ruggedness is its main character along with the intriguing quarry of Hodge Close with its aqueduct, lake, man-made holes and tunnels. The highlight is the great arch, which to the novice should be observed rather than explored, for be warned, deaths have occurred here in climbing its extreme routes with divers and swimmers also being caught in the flooded chambers. The summit of naked rock provides a grand view of Coniston Water and is the cherry on the cake of this delightful fell.

Lesser in stature but not in strength,
Roguishly rugged, rough along its length,
Juniper, heather, fern, those tough tangled shrubs,
Colourful slate quarry, the arches at hub,
A Lakeland mountain through and through,
Shows Coniston Water shining striking view.

HOPEGILL HEAD

Region: North West **Height:** 2,526 ft **Grid Ref:** NY185221

Hopegill Head summit is exhilarating and is dominated by the precipitous cliff face that goes by the name of Hobcarton Crag (locals, by the way, sometimes call this fell Hobcarton Pike). Often climbed as part of the Coledale round, this pointed peak gives wide-ranging views with even the Isle of Man and the Scottish Border hills seen on a clear day. The crag may look like a good place for climbers but the crumbly slate makes this highly dangerous and often only frozen winter sport takes place here.

Swinside to Ladyside,
For Hopegill Head,
Sharp twists contortions,
Shaping rocky beds.

Shattered slate decorates,
Airy ranging summit peak,
Shouting ravens make a din,
Those noisy creaking beaks.

Flying out from the face,
Floating on wind they bind,
And here we stand on ruinous brink,
With humbled state of mind.

ILL BELL

Region: Far East **Height:** 2,484 ft **Grid Ref:** NY436078

Standing on a narrow ridge between two valleys Ill Bell is easy to spot as from most directions the mountain appears as a conical bell shape. The eastern flank is a rough cove and is in contrast to the western side which although still steep is smooth. The paths here run along to the nearby fell of Froswick which mirrors its mightier neighbour in shape giving the whole ridge a rollercoaster look. There are several large columnar cairns on the summit that make the fell even more recognisable. The view up here of Windermere and Scafell is really good.

The grand dome of Ill Bell tolls,
Here dominating conical mount unfolds,
Sheer slopes plunge, valleys surround,
Conquered from Troutbeck or Kentmere ground
Rise strong to pinnacle that nature made tough,
Fear the heart of the mountain so ragged so rough.

ILLGILL HEAD (WASTWATER SCREES)

Region: South **Height:** 1,998 ft **Grid Ref:** NY169049

A visit to Wastwater is highly recommended. On its south-eastern shore the lake is walled in by a vast run of falling scree that continues far into the deepest lake in England. On top of this wall the flat platform summit of Illgill Head can be found, although when standing here you really have no clue to the drama along its edge. The view of Wasdale Head from the summit cairn is fine and with care, following the paths nearby to the west, there are places where you can see over and down onto the dramatic scree and lake itself.

From mountain top to lake below,
Where Scafell range cools its toes,
Here drama falls to plunging depths,
The loose and shifting rocky edge,
The spectacle of stone-strewn flank,
Unique in England's pleasant ranks,
Reflected in water's transparent glass,
Nature's so violent eroding past.

KENTMERE PIKE

Region: Far East **Height:** 2,395 ft **Grid Ref:** NY465078

This fell is normally taken in while doing the Kentmere round, but again like similar horseshoe routes the best side of the mountain is missed. Far better to approach from the Longsleddale valley where the mountain shows a craggy face and an interesting quarry in the form of Wrengill. The summit, a grassy dome, encompasses changeable views with the vista of Lakeland hidden then revealed in the gaps through neighbouring mountains. However, to the south the panorama opens up and Windermere comes into view.

What sheer violence was rendered,
To mountainside so tame and tender?
In valley of Longsleddale a stone hard vice,
Goat Scar, Raven Crag, Steel Pike.

Rocks rain down like savage fists,
Here gorge of River Sprint turns, twists,
This side of mount profuse, profound,
In contrast fully gentle Kentmere ground.

KIDSTY PIKE

Region: Far East **Height:** 2,559 ft **Grid Ref:** NY447126

On a clear day Kidsty Pike sticks out like a sore thumb with its sharp angled peak leaving walkers in no doubt of the location. Also, travellers along the M6 often notice this high point and pass it daily on the way to work never having trod its paths or known its name. The fell can be climbed directly only from the shore of Haweswater at Mardale Head. The view from the summit is somewhat curtailed by High Street and its neighbours, but the Straits of Riggindale reward.

Haweswater ghosts cry,
Riggingdale ruins rise,
Hi ho, Howes,
Path to clouds.

Southern skies skirt,
Prominent profile perched,
Fells formed feature,
Famous Lakeland creature.

KIRK FELL

Region: West Height: 2,631 ft Grid Ref: NY195104

Kirk Fell is often stated in guidebooks as not all that appealing to the walker. I think this is a very harsh assessment and this jumping on a negative bandwagon is mainly on account of its really steep paths and bracken slopes. They are steep, no doubt about that, but after all, this is a mountain and one of the tallest in the district, God forbid we should actually have to "climb" a mountain to get to the top! Cynicism aside, the fell has a lot going for it. Kirk Fell Crags are its main feature and certainly catch the eye. So do the views here from the summit as Great Gable is seen in fantastic profile showing wonderfully The Napes and Gable Crag. Over Wasdale the Scafell range is seen from end to end so it is certainly worth the hard slog.

Forgotten guardian of Wasdale Head,
As multitudes flock to Great Gable instead,
For bracken and grass cannot really compete,
With good solid rock beneath your feet.

Though all is not lost without a moment of doubt,
Kirk Fell Crags a challenge to hardily mount,
Steep though the climb and so heavy the sweat,
Rewarded by view that is not your debt.

KNOTT

Region: North Height: 2,392 ft Grid Ref: NY296329

Knott simply means hill in old Cumbrian and although this fell lacks the drama of hard rock the smooth gentle grass slopes have their own brand of beauty. This place has a drawback though as it is one of the most unfrequented tops due to its accessibility. No roads or major paths can be found nearby and it requires a long walk over the moor top to reach the summit. The view here is changeable; the blander sides of Blencathra and Skiddaw block most of the foreground but glimpses of Thirlmere and mountains to the south can be seen. To the north the Scottish hills and the Solway Firth dominate the panorama.

Into serenity of the Northern wilderness,
The miles of moorland waste unfold,
The long and narrow grassy routes test,
Test not the body but the soul.

Alone you stand as the wind whispers,
Voices drift on the breeze to the ear,
You look all around to see speaker,
But only the sheep are here.

KNOTT RIGG

Region: North West Height 1,824 ft Grid Ref: NY197188

Knott Rigg, standing at the head of the Newlands valley, is usually easily climbed on the way to the adjoining fell of Ard Crags. I say easily climbed as the often used car park starting point at Newlands Hause is situated nearly halfway up! The view from the summit is restricted mainly because of the higher Coledale and Buttermere fells nearby. However, a view does open up towards the Skiddaw and Helvellyn ranges.

Warden of quiet valley so fair,
Road leads to the summit stair,
Knott Rigg an easy one hour cause,
Adventure begun at Newlands Hause,
Gentle the summit walk over verdant top,
Eye drawn to Helvellyn and the Dodds.

THE KNOTT

Region: Far East **Height:** 2,425 ft **Grid Ref:** NY436127

The Knott is one of the high points on Rampsgill Head and is often climbed with High Street in mind via the zigzag route from Hayeswater reservoir. When climbed from this direction the fell looks quite impressive with its conical shape and deep gully. On reaching the top though its inferiority can be seen when compared to its parent fell. The view is far from inferior here with grand vistas opening up to the west. Ullswater and Brothers Water can be brought into the view by just moving along the summit slightly to the south-west.

From Low Hartsop to high Hayeswater,
Path to High Street does not falter,
Twisting, turning steep zigzag path,
Deep scree fan gully shows its wrath,
The Knott is key to many a route,
More ridge and pass to test your boots.

LANK RIGG

Region: West **Height:** 1,775 ft **Grid Ref:** NY092119

Remote on the southern fringe of this region, the mountains turn from rock to gentle rolling hillsides and green grass. You will not meet many a walker hereabouts as this fell is well away from the usual suspects, but Lank Rigg is without a doubt a beautiful place to roam if you want peace and quiet. Best ascended from the Coldfell Road the summit provides an adequate view of Lakeland with Blencathra in the distance. Visitors here may find coins hidden under rocks, a tradition inspired by Alfred Wainright – who else?

Isolated, lonely,
Solitary height,
Boundary outlier,
Unfrequented type.

Rewarding, restful,
Pastoral grace,
Running waters,
Gaining pace.

LATRIGG

Region: North Height: 1,207 ft Grid Ref: NY279247

One of those lesser height gems that is very much admired due to its beautiful summit views being truly excellent. It also helps that Latrigg is close to Keswick town, so is very conveniently visited. Wooded on the lower slopes, the heights are grassy pastures with little rock. But this fell is all about the southern panorama. Derwentwater and the town almost go unnoticed as the horizon erupts, drawing the eye towards the many mountain summit peaks.

Keswick townsfolk have come to love,
Junior fell of famous Skiddaw club,
Pure natural charm makes heart well,
Sunday walkers, lovers, all will tell.

Of the gentle nature, the stunning view,
The gem of the district waiting for you
On the horizon mountain peaks abrupt.
Derwentwater afore – reflections conduct.

LING FELL

Region: North West **Height:** 1,224 ft **Grid Ref:** NY179286

Ling Fell is pleasant enough to look at, has good views of the Galloway Hills and is easily accessible from Wythop Mill. The fell itself though can be heavy going at certain times of the year when the gorse and bracken are growing thick. Paths are rare adding to the difficulties of ascent though one route can be found that leads up the valley and contours round to the north before hitting the summit. Grouse butts can be found over the hillside, the remains of old country sport.

No ridges to ride,
No crags to climb,
No glorious rock,
No summit that's fine.

Dark heather looks gloomy,
Bracken fern bars the day,
Gorse grass wide patches,
Clothes solitary sloped way.

LINGMELL

Region: South **Height:** 2,648 ft **Grid Ref:** NY209081

Lingmell is a well-known stepping stone to Scafell Pike but it is more than a convenient outlier on the way to the highest mountain in England. The fell has those two opposing faces often seen in the Lakes, the easy sloped side versus the utter rocky devastation. The main distinguishing feature is the craggy face and the dark gorge just below Piers Gill that has water running into its depths from the heights of the Scafells. The summit claims to have the best view of Great Gable and in my opinion is wrongly bypassed in the hurry to the Scafells.

Two faces of Lingmell, north–south contradiction,
Mountain of character shown in distinction,
Gentle the giant rises, topped grassy plateau,
Deadly the giant falls, craggy confusion below.

Desolate, decaying destruction of thousand-foot declination,
Accentuated by profusion poured devastations,
The cleft of Piers Gill collects in its boots,
In choked channels and courses perilous to foot.

On other shoulder lies Brown Tongue
Well-worn route to England's high rung,
Where grand elevations are the norm,
Unparalleled, savage beauties in their form.

LINGMOOR FELL

Region: South **Height:** 1,539 ft **Grid Ref:** NY302046

Lingmoor Fell stands amidst the better known fells of the Langdale and Coniston groups but is attached to neither, standing alone with no connecting ridges to other heights. The mountain is, and has been, a real provider for man with slate and timber taken from its slopes which also provide quality pasture for many sheep. The views from the summit are glorious all round with the classic sight of Harrison Stickle seen from a higher than normal angle.

From low pleasant pleasing pastures
And well-wooded path-ridden vale,
Rises a curving crescent unassuming fell,
Generous, prosperous, yielding natural worth,
Giving up timber and Cumbrian green stone,
Nurturing, nursing romping lambs in spring,
Freely giving inspiration to the solitary poets,
And famous vantages of well-defined vista,
A Magnus Opus, a great work for all to behold.

LITTLE HART CRAG

Region: East **Height:** 2,090 ft **Grid Ref:** NY387100

At the head of Scandale is Little Hart Crag, an outlier of Dove Crag and often climbed as part of the Fairfield Horseshoe route. The summit has two distinct tops which give good views of the nearby crags of the parent fell and Red Screes, but the rest of the panorama is slightly restricted. Most routes to the top start from Brothers Water in Patterdale via other fells, there being no distinct direct way.

Proud sentinel of Scandale Pass,
Watching, waiting, anticipating,
The valley of Hartsop's generations,
The comings and goings of the lucky few,
To walk hidden beauty in Hoggett Gill,
To stand still contemplating praises,
Hearing voices on the blowing breeze.

LITTLE MELL FELL

Region: East **Height:** 1,657 ft **Grid Ref:** NY423240

Often seen from the main roads but rarely climbed is Great Mell Fell's twin sister, Little Mell Fell. The domed summit has a good view towards the Eastern fells but the foreground is hindered by the wide, curved grassy top. Watch out for adders, the occasional sign says so be careful where you sit for your picnic! The fell is virtually pathless and care should be taken regarding rights of access from the lower slopes. The car parking spaces at the Hause are the safest starting point.

Standing alone the lesser twin,
Marker portal to the end and the begin,
For here mountains fall to the wide stretching plain,
The fell barely touched except by wind and the rain.

LOADPOT HILL

Region: Far East **Height:** 2,205 ft **Grid Ref:** NY457181

There is more to Loadpot Hill than might first appear to the eye. First, it covers a huge swath of ground and second, within this area the fell delivers many delights, especially of historic interest. In the Moor Divock area the hand of ancient man can be found in the form of stone circles, tumuli, standing stones and boundary posts. Old quarries and sink wells can also be found. The remains of an old hunting lodge called Lowther House sits near the summit and the course of the Roman road of High Street runs over the mountain to Penrith. The view as you move round the summit area is excellent especially towards Western Lakeland.

Loadpot Hill vast extensive range,
Gradually dispenses to moorland grass plain,
The rock only showing at Ullswater's wake,
Which its waters feed and the Lowther make.

Ancient hand of man abounds,
Standing stones in profusion bound,
Moor Divock where you find the most,
Though don't be fooled by boundary posts.

The summit is flat but the view is princely,
Nearby to south remains Lowther House chimney,
Roman High Street traverses verdant top,
Follow road to adventures that never stop!

LOFT CRAG

Region: Central **Height:** 2,238 ft **Grid Ref** NY277071

Loft Crag is a familiar old friend to me, as it was in Great Langdale as a child that I first climbed the Langdale Pikes from the National Trust campsite. I still have great adventures here to this day and some of my fondest memories are both physical and romantically spiritual. This fell sits amongst its contemporaries with a craggy look on its face, a wise old master that does not quite get the press of say Harrison Stickle or Pike O'Stickle but it is still very well known, especially to the climbing community, many of whom have taken their first steps on Gimmer Crag. Teachers and students can be found taking a well-earned beer in the Old Dungeon Ghyll Hotel bar where many an adventure grows in stature after a few pints!

One of Langdale's proud complement,
Companion of rocky might,
Firmly stuck between the middle,
Pike O'Stickle and Harrison heights.

Your buttress of Gimmer Crag
A proving ground of training climbers,
Generations learnt their skills here,
Led up face by veteran old timers.

LONG SIDE

Region: North **Height: 2,**408 ft **Grid Ref:** NY248284

Long Side is often climbed on the way to Skiddaw along the continuation of the ridge that runs up from the initial first stage of Ullock Pike, then running along the famous Longside Edge before joining up with the higher Carl Side, the last stage to the grand prize. This is without doubt a most thrilling walk with wonderful inspiring views of Bassenthwaite Lake. The huge bulk of Skiddaw is seen ahead to the east and blocks out almost all the vista in this direction.

A lofty leap is Long Side,
High-level inspiring ledge,
Shadows fall deep into valley,
Down from the rough steep edge.

The aromatic summit smells,
Heather, mosses, bilberry too,
Add to that glorious collection,
Choicest classic Cumbrian view.

LONGLANDS FELL

Region: North **Height:** 1,585 ft **Grid Ref:** NY275353

The Uldale Fells is a quiet part of the National Park which is mainly made up of gentle grassland, an ideal sheep pasture. Visible rock is a rarity as is any history of mining (unlike the neighbouring Caldbecks) with the failed Longlands Fell copper works the only mine in the area. The heights mark a passive but still beautiful finish to Lakeland and provide really good views to the north and south, and west to the sea.

The end of Lakeland is found here,
As mountains give way to lesser ground,
The foothills not rocky, mainly just turf,
Extend to Scotland and Solway Firth,
Longlands has merit despite pleasant ease,
Northern vista presence so certain to please.

LONSCALE FELL

Region: North **Height:** 2,346 ft **Grid Ref:** NY285272

Lonscale Fell is a well-recognised subsidiary of Skiddaw as its second summit and has a distinctive pointed end. The mountain on its eastern approaches was once heavily mined, but the main industry now is sheep farming with fair pasture available to graze. There are quite a few routes to the summit but many take advantage of the high situated Gale Road car park behind Latrigg. The view is restricted with the Northern fells being so close but to the south a fine vista is displayed with Thirlmere and Derwentwater nestled between some major ranges.

Sharp climax grabs the sky,
Graceful gentle on the eye,
Paths here are not hard to handle,
Except north-east ridge buttress scramble,
The summit tower of fair east peak
Provides best viewpoint from two thousand feet.

LORD'S SEAT

Region: North West **Height:** 1.811 ft **Grid Ref:** NY204265

The lower slopes of Lord's Seat are extensively forested, where huge plantations changing in size, shape and colour come and go over the years, each forest with its own name. The fell is the highest in this area hence the name. The rough but fun scramble of Barf can be found on its main ridge with Broom Fell and Graystones nearby. The domed summit is clear of trees and provides quite an extensive view over Bassenthwaite to the Northern fells.

Lord's Seat sits defined in the Lakeland nation,
In vast dark woods and named below plantations,
Here paths and roads are walked with open permission,
As the operations are run by the Forestry Commission.

Beckstones, Darling How, Aiken too,
Whinlatter, Hospital, Swinside,Comb,
Hobcarton and the by the lake Wythop Wood,
The summit though is open, trees withstood.

LOUGHRIGG FELL

Region: Central **Height:** 1,099 ft **Grid Ref:** NY347051

Loughrigg is one of those small gems, most likely the best of them all. I would get lynched for saying otherwise but I do not need my arm twisted to extol its many virtues! The fell has everything going for it: history, location, sylvan scenes in abundance from top to bottom, and a brilliant view is the cherry on the cake. Wordsworth country always inspires!

Grand stature alone does not measure mountains' worth,
And so it truly stands with Loughrigg, of lesser heights,
If love made tall loftiness, then fell would be of might.

For benevolent love this ridge and mass endears,
Footfalls testament declared in many paths laid,
Leading wealth, natures worth, earnest grace have made.

Find a poetic peace of mind visiting Rydal Water
Treading hallowed routes, The Terrace amongst the fore,
Footfalls on velvet grass carpets, rich bracken-lined floors.

Promise is found on passage to summit that never deceives,
For the famous fells of Lakeland three hundred & sixty degrees surround,
Such blessed beauty displays the humble elevation's crown.

LOW FELL

Region: West **Height:** 1,388 ft **Grid Ref:** NY137226

Certainly not in the same league as Loughrigg but still worthy nonetheless for the clear views on offer and these alone make the sometimes steep climb up Low Fell worth the effort. The fell, you will notice, has many enclosures but these rarely hinder your way to the top with the easiest ascent being from Thackthwaite in Lorton valley.

Diminutive pinnacle a guilty pleasure,
Another small height to secretly treasure,
For seen from summit is a vision grand,
Crummock, Buttermere, set in mountain bands.

LOW PIKE

Region: East **Height:** 1,667 ft **Grid Ref:** NY373077

Low Pike is the first fell from Ambleside en route to the Fairfield Horseshoe – look for the signs to Low Sweden Bridge and you're on the path to this popular round. The summit has a small rocky finish to it and does require a slight scramble. The views are very good especially of the town and the head of Windermere with Langdale and Coniston putting on a good show. But otherwise the closer grander heights restrict the view.

First stepping stone of Fairfield way,
The horseshoe round of Ambleside sway,
To Low Sweden path, you earnestly head,
Crossing the bridge spanning Scandale Beck,
Then follow the wall for a mile or more,
Up spine of the ridge for summit tor.

MAIDEN MOOR

Region: North West **Height:** 1,890 ft **Grid Ref:** NY236182

Maiden Moor is an excellent viewpoint but good luck finding the exact summit due to its elevation being a large rounded grassy topped plateau. The views up here are excellent, it must be said, especially of the Newlands valley towards the Coledale fells and Derwentwater way to Keswick. Beatrix Potter has some history here too for the home of Mrs Tiggy-winkle is nearby just above the old Yewthwaite lead mine!

From Little Town way a three-tier cake,
Knott End, High Crag, the grass summit make,
Top a little plain, though there's a super place to stand,
Checkout Newlands Edge from bull-nosed overhang.

MARDALE ILL BELL

Region: Far East **Height:** 2,493 ft **Grid Ref:** NY448102

The most climbed way up this fell is from Mardale itself, taking in a popular pass and impressive scenery with high waters. Mardale Ill Bell is situated on the south-east ridge of High Street and although the view up here is slightly restricted by Ill Bell itself, the Coniston panoramas are well seen. The true gems though are the views of the Mardale waters from the rim of crags.

At north-east face blandness duly altered,
Volcanic craters stunning Mardale waters,
Piot Crag, old quarry from the past,
A grand noted feature, Nan Bield pass,
At Small Water shelters once were made,
Travellers, tradesmen flat in them laid.

MEAL FELL

Region: North **Height:** 1,804 ft **Grid Ref:** NY282337

Visiting the Lake District you are bound to see a lot sheep, and as previously mentioned the outlying Northern regions make great pasture with many Herdwicks present! Normally there is little rock in these parts, though Meal Fell has a rare outcrop on the summit. There is also the possibility that another hill fort along the lines of Carrock Fell may have been here, the scant evidence being what is thought to be a quarried circle around the summit knoll. Views of Lakeland are quite restricted but towards the sea the panorama opens up.

The trodden track up to Trusmadoor,
Is started from the low Longlands floor,
Without a shadow of a doubt the best way to go,
Especially for shepherds with sheep in flow,
A rare rocky summit amongst Uldale heights,
Where your eyes will be drawn to seaward sights.

MELLBREAK

Region: North West **Height:** 1,680 ft **Grid Ref:** NY148186

Mellbreak, despite being surrounded by grander fells, is a true rarity in that it stands alone. The fell is a real treat too as it runs along the shores of Crummock Water and although modest in elevation the sudden steepness of its slopes gives it a much recognised eye-catching profile. The views from both its north and south summit cairns are very good indeed with the former having the addition of the Solway Firth. Grasmoor, across the lake, impressively dominates.

Teeming with life round stony shores,
Crummock Water so well adored,
Set against blissful blessed scene,
Dark stark steepness boldly intervenes,
Fast ascending soaring sky high,
Look at me! it shouts, it cries,
Fiercely independent standing alone,
Highly recommended to romp and roam,
So follow the path from Kirkhead Farm,
Steep rise on edge holds adventure and charm.

MIDDLE DODD

Region: East **Height:** 2,146 ft **Grid Ref:** NY397096

When ascending Kirkstone Pass from Ullswater this fell can be seen to your right and is rarely climbed in truth for its own sake being an outlier of the Helvellyn range and a stepping stone to Red Screes. The views though from the summit are really good which is surprising considering the closeness of grander heights. The route up the nose of the fell is very steep. In fact most of the paths here are really punishment but they do provide direct ascents.

Often viewed by motorised sightseers,
Low geared climbing up famous Kirkstone Pass,
Only ascended by many people in their minds,
As the rocks and boulders rumble past.

The few, the worthy, aspire to summit,
Putting real effort into hiking up harsh slopes.
They are rewarded with open Scafell views,
Showing this mount is no forlorn hope.

MIDDLE FELL

Region: West **Height:** 1,909 ft **Grid Ref:** NY151072

Standing above the northern shore of Wastwater this fell can be climbed from Greendale. It is an excellent viewpoint for those after a great experience of the lake and the famous screes that drop so dramatically into its depths. The ascent is steep as the harsh slope rides up the nose of the ridge but once conquered, paths can be continued onto the satellite fell of Seatallan.

Robust ruggedness,
Hostile heights,
Perfect platform,
Panoramic sights.

Picture vista,
Veritable rapture,
Manifest, majestic,
Wastwater captured.

MUNGRISDALE COMMON

Region: North **Height:** 2,077 ft **Grid Ref:** NY312292

If Mungrisdale Common was down south it would be a much admired and famous fell without a doubt! Here though amongst an embarrassment of riches this mount is seen as a bland, wet, tufty grass blob. Harsh but true with one saving grace – the view of course. A place for peak baggers only. You have been warned and I make no apologies for the poem!

Really a boring bland grass waste,
Only Wainwright baggers here make haste,
That along with hungry Herdwick sheep,
Their plentiful droppings found in heaps!

NAB SCAR

Region: East Height: 1,493 ft Grid Ref: NY356073

It's a controversial statement to say that Nab Scar is the beginning not the end of the Fairfield Horseshoe, but there I said it here in black and white! Not only is it the first stepping stone on that famous route but the slopes have also been home to our famous poets, me included! Moving on swiftly, I am no William Wordsworth nor would I claim to be. His poetry was for a different age and more elegant audience, whilst mine is for every man, the everyday Wainwright walker. I, however, pay slight homage to Wordsworth's style in this poem; it seemed the right thing to do as I sat on the shore of Rydal Water. Oh, by the way, the views up top are extensive, especially to the nearby Central fells, with these putting on a bold front.

Many have been charmed.....many have wandered,
Wandered in wide wonderment on sylvan shores,
Where tree-lined slopes rise to commanding seat,
Those many inspired by vibrant verdant visions,
Entering rich romances, soul spirited dreams,
True Heaven on Earth and so right does it seem.

THE NAB

Region: Far East **Height:** 1,890 ft **Grid Ref:** NY434152

Finally opened up by the Rights of Way Act 2000, The Nab is one of those fells just for the peak bagger. Approaches are now allowed by the Estate in Martindale because of the aforementioned act but don't expect a warm welcome, expect to be questioned en route. I was twice. Best to go the traditionalist Wainwright way via Rest Dodd, the fell usually being a slight diversion, a tick in a box, en route to or from High Street. The view is not the best as it is often obstructed by higher ground, although Helvellyn makes a show.

Avoid risky Martindale, the wrath of Estate,
For walkers and campers they seem to rarely tolerate,
Walking through deer park is perceived as harm,
In truth grassy dome summit holds very little charm,
Rest Dodd, for the baggers, old long way to go,
The progress over peat bogs is soggy and slow.

NETHERMOST PIKE

Region: East Height: 2,923 ft Grid Ref: NY343142

Nethermost Pike is a grand mountain especially from its eastern approaches. Helvellyn takes from its fame of course, but footfall here is still heavy, whether coming to or from the master of the range. Unfortunately for this mountain most of the multitude start on easy paths from Wythburn traversing the slopes here and making a beeline for Helvellyn, never reaching the summit or seeing the grand sights on offer. I have said it before and I will say it again, always best to approach this range from the east, where the paths are quieter and the drama of the rock more exhilarating. Please take care though as this area has a lot of rare flora that should not be disturbed and is protected by a Site of Special Scientific Interest (S.S.S.I). The summit views are truly excellent!

Thousands throng from Wythburn way,
Especially on those bank holidays in May,
I for one prefer less frequented paths,
With rock and ridge a scramble to grasp.

Adventurous routes can be taken,
Grisedale routes, hard graft in making,
Up the valley on to Nethermost Cove,
Then up East Ridge and on we go!

OUTERSIDE

Region: North West **Height:** 1,995 ft **Grid Ref:** NY211214

Outerside is one of the smaller members of the Coledale group but is quite distinctive in shape showing a conical profile from most directions. The fell is crowded in slightly by larger fells and this somewhat restricts the view but the mountains surrounding it are interesting as is the view of the valley. The Hellvellyn range can also be seen to good effect. The ridge off Outerside leads to the much loved Barrow.

Abrupt steep from abyss,
Rising out of Coledale mists,
Outerside the lonely fell,
Rare visitors have tales to tell,
For though view is hemmed in tight,
Gasp at raw close up intimate sights.

PAVEY ARK

Region: Central **Height:** 2,279 ft **Grid Ref:** NY285079

I have a lot of love for Pavey Ark. This mount has a lot going for it; it is part of the Langdale Pikes and has an interesting approach in the form of Stickle Ghyll with waterfalls that lead up to Stickle Tarn, a lovely corrie that sits in front of the sheer face of the fell. Quite the eye opener as the view is only revealed at the last moment adding to the drama. A cleft called Jack's Rake runs up the face right to left and is a grade 1 scramble. Although unexposed in its early stages it becomes more dangerous as you proceed, needing you to have a head for heights. There are several chimney and gully challenges for full-on climbers and this area is often used for training novices as well

Welcome to the scenic sensation,
Langdales' lauded playground cliff,
Where masses swarm from valley,
Up the Stickle Ghyll well-worn stair lift.

The sight that greets them,
Having wearily reached the tarn,
Is one of vivid striking drama,
Behind water's delicate charm.

There is something about this mystical crag,
Days are spent wondering at its blessed grace,
Others seize the challenge set,
And scramble up cleft in its face.

Jack's Rake is not for everyone,
Beware! Beware! Beware!
Some poor souls have lost their lives,
Use due diligence and climb with care.

PIKE O'BLISCO

Region: South Height: 2,313 ft Grid Ref: NY271042

Pike O'Blisco is the guardian watching from on high the entrance to Little Langdale from Great Langdale. Standing a little aloof from the main attractions of Crinkle Crags and Bowfell this mountain is often climbed en route to these famous heights. The fell has that classic mountain shape leading up steep slopes to the pointed peak, the shape that demands you climb it. The view from the summit is excellent, the stars of the show being nearby. But if you can draw your eyes away from them, there are other grand sights to see as you walk round the summit.

A romping romance and adventure unfolds,
For the rugged flanks of Pike O'Blisco awaits,
This grand enterprise in splendid stature,
Standing in strength, sturdiness, calls you,
Your company it frankly craves, challenge set,
Its abundant craggy massif lays gauntlet down,
So pick up the grey glove, earn spurs on path,
Seek true endeavours earnest quest.

PIKE O'STICKLE

Region: Central **Height:** 2,326 ft **Grid Ref:** NY273073

As with the majority of the Langdale Pikes this fell is easily recognised, its front sweeping up from the valley below to the dome-shaped summit peak. The narrow scree run from Stickle Stone Shoot is also a noted feature and over the years has yielded several Langdale stoStone Age axes from the cave factory near the top. The view is excellent towards the south but Bowfell opposite steals the show.

Are some mountains made of magic?
Are they conjured by mystical arts?
Are they shaped by affable wizards
With man's adventures close to their hearts?

In the enchanted vale of Mickleden,
Stands such a peak, a bell-shaped pike,
The soaring thrust from valley to summit,
Oh you have never seen its like!

Even the ancients understood its power,
Making tools from spiritual rocks,
The grand axes so much sought after,
Mined and manufactured near hallowed top.

PILLAR

Region: West **Height:** 2,927 ft **Grid Ref:** Y171121

Pillar is the birthplace of rock climbing in the Lake District with its origins centred on the prominent feature known as Pillar Rock. Not exclusively the territory of the climber, this fell is excellent scrambling and walking country too and a visit to Pillar is exhilarating. The High Level Route to the summit is a "must do" walk; the path is narrow but wide enough for a safe traverse and gives the impression from a distance of being a lot worse than it actually turns out to be. The poem describes the route to take. Views from the summit are excellent with almost all the major mountain ranges on display with the exception of Coniston.

Adventure your first, middle and last name,
The High Level Route should be your game,
Black Sail to viewpoint on Looking Stead,
Now you can see the drama ahead.

Green Cove route to Robinson's Cairn
Here is the Shamrock, it will do no harm,
With care make your way, to see Pillar Rock,
DO NOT ATTEMPT!
Unless made of good climbing stock.

Here lies Pisgah, High and Low Man,
Dramatically down to Ennerdale they span,
Where you'll spend time, gazing in awe,
Mind marvelling, the adrenalin soars.

Now for the summit, tough scramble up scree,
It's so worth the effort, every footfall sweaty,
For summit shows mountains grandly presented,
With adventure today be so well contented.

PLACE FELL

Region: Far East **Height:** 2,156 ft **Grid Ref:** NY405169

Place Fell is one of those mountains that is a real joy, and thanks to its location alongside Ullswater it is perfectly placed! The path along the shoreline at its foot is one of the best walks in the district, where the western flanks fall steeply and add to the wonderful scenery. The heights should not be ignored and are full of Lakeland character. The view, especially across the water up past Patterdale and Glenridding towards Helvellyn is very striking.

This fell, this country, location favours,
Full mountain character in plentiful measures,
The rugged rough tumble, the bracken, the heather,
Forgotten paths, ancient cairns, old ruins, lost treasure.

Here few better lakeside paths, Ullswater unfolds,
That curves around the shore in God's miracle mould,
Sandwick to Silver Point the grandest line,
An honour to walk that rewards most fine.

RAISE

Region: East **Height:** 2,897 ft **Grid Ref:** NY342174

Raise is one of the mountains on the main Helvellyn ridge and is often visited en route to the parent fell. It isn't the most exciting of summits as the fell is made up mainly of grassy slopes easing up either side to the heights, via the east–west route of Sticks Pass, but the top does have a small rocky outcrop. The summit view is excellent all round with all the major groups on show. The area known as Savages Gully provides good skiing country of a sorts and the Lake District Ski Club operates a nearly 1000 ft. long lift here.

Rising gently from east and west,
Sticks Pass on shoulder of Raise behest,
A quick way to ascend Helvellyn heights,
Saving some energy for ridge walk delights,
And when winter has frozen grip on vales,
Skiers glide down on snow white sails.

RAMPSGILL HEAD

Region: Far East **Height:** 2,598 ft **Grid Ref:** NY443128

Forming a meeting of three ridges Rampsgill Head is a focal point west of Haweswater and for such a high fell occupies only a small area being hemmed in by Kidsty Pike, High Street and The Knott. The northern face drops dramatically down over 1,800 feet and is the main feature of the fell. The view is a good one especially westwards towards Ullswater.

Debris scatters down.....

Boulders tumble crashing round.....

Here the fringe falls.....

Hayeswater shores....... call.

RANNERDALE KNOTTS

Region: North West **Height:** 1,165 ft **Grid Ref:** NY167182

In the side valley of Rannerdale the bluebells grow in profusion during April and May. It is a beautiful sight but according to local folklore the flowers sprang from the spilt blood of Norman invaders ambushed by the Saxons from the heights of Rannerdale Knotts. This fell is one of the smaller ones on the Wainwrights list but it has much going for it, rising from Buttermere Valley with excellent views across Crummock Water but being dominated by nearby giants.

The springtime hue is a stunning sea of blue,
Best visited when the dawning sunshine hits the dew.
Green the oasis where medieval blood once flowed,
Killing Norman invaders with victory bestowed,
Springing surprise, ambush! Revenge begot,
Here on short sweet mountain, Rannerdale Knotts.

RAVEN CRAG

Region: Central **Height:** 1,512 ft **Grid Ref:** NY304188

Raven Crag is a great little platform for an aerial view of Thirlmere but the rest of the vista is hemmed in by trees and higher mountains. The main crag has a 500-foot sheer drop, often frequented by climbers, but steep paths around this can be taken (the ground can be quite marshy and wet). A visit to the nearby Iron Age fort earthworks on Castle Crag (no relation to the famous Borrowdale one!) can add to this little adventure.

Rising from dense dark forest,
Your slopes marshy ground,
Thirlmere mighty buttress,
Standing proud, sheer face found.

The summit view of waters grand,
Down to south end and up to dam,
Do not attempt the craggy face,
It's a solely roped up climbers' place.

RED PIKE (BUTTERMERE)

Region: West Height: 2,477 ft Grid Ref: NY160154

Of the two Red Pikes it is this one in the Buttermere valley that deserves the name, chiefly because of its colour! Both fells, although quite close to each other, are very different entities but I shall not enter into the argument as to which one is better as they are in my opinion both great. This Red Pike summit has great views and is famous for being able to see a good number of lakes. The ridge walk that heads to Haystacks is one of the finest found in Lakeland.

A most popular Buttermere valley hike,
The route of rock up buttressed pike,
Here the stone is rich bloody red,
As the syenite runs through the soil bed.

The view's a classic with many lakes seen,
And the mountain itself in Adam's Ale teems,
For water here is the star attraction,
Varying in type with pleasant reactions.

The cascading course flows of Sour Milk Gill
To the beautiful falls of Scale Force thrill,
And not forgetting the hidden volcano yarn,
In the deep dark depths of Bleaberry Tarn.

RED PIKE (WASDALE)

Region: West **Height:** 2,710 ft **Grid Ref:** NY165105

This Red Pike isn't red as such like its namesake but has the distinction of being higher and has an almost continuous run of crags above Mosedale. This fell is also part of a famous ridge walk called the Mosedale Horseshoe which takes in Pillar as well as others. The summit, with its large cairn, has another interesting feature in the form of the The Chair, an armchair-shaped wind shelter from where grand views can be seen of Scafell and the Wasdale Screes.

Exhilarating escarpment,
Terrific traverse,
Declining declivities,
Extravagant earth.

Pinnacle precipice,
Spiritual space,
Shocking senses,
Profound grace.

RED SCREES

Region: East **Height:** 2,546 ft **Grid Ref:** NY396087

Red Screes is a pilgrimage point for me on my adventures round the lakes, not because it's a famous grand height or that it has any really arresting features as such, although the still-worked Kirkstone Quarry grabs the eye and sometimes the ears as well when they are blasting. Mainly I love it for its incredible summit view (this is one of those windy summits), which spans 360 degrees around and also down to the welcome sight of the Kirky – the Kirkstone Pass Inn from whose car park I have scrambled up the eastern face to the pinnacle. The pub sits at the grand height of 1500 feet – I know it's cheating and I have disapproved of it elsewhere in this guidebook but here there is a beer involved! You will have earned a pie and pint on the very steep 1000-foot scramble but not before. I said not before!!

Dark runs your blood in rock and stone,
That are whipped by winds that chill to bone,
Lord of Lords in high Kirkstone Pass,
Where grass gives way to quarry and shaft,
Ascending from inn is sheer and steep,
An adventurous scramble hard to beat,
Rewarding summit views not to be missed,
So best not to climb in rain or a mist.

REST DODD

Region: Far East **Height:** 2,283 ft **Grid Ref:** NY432137

Wainwright was not a fan of this fell but I felt he was a little harsh. Yes, the summit is a bit bland but certain views from here are excellent, especially of the Helvellyn range and northward towards Rampsgill valley. The scree slope on the eastern side is also of interest falling dramatically down in colourful runs.

Solitary summit stand of Rest Dodd,
The less frequented heights, left untrod,
Where scree roams abounding round dome,
And even the sheep here do not roam,
On eastern falling flank of many colours,
Stone showing cast, seen in full light of summer.

ROBINSON

Region: North West **Height:** 2,418 ft **Grid Ref:** NY201118

Robinson is one of those fells often climbed in the mind from the car, as the Newlands road runs along its flankSome will park the car and head off to the heights. Moss Force, the waterfall seen from below, is well worth a visit close up and for the best view from the heights head to High Snockrigg for excellent views of Buttermere. This fell can be very wet in places so be prepared to get soggy boots. Most of the major fells are in sight from the summit although the foreground is robbed by the wide plateau.

Course tumbles,
Full flow,
Moss Force,
Waters grow,
Down falls,
Newlands Hause,
Road side,
Pictorial pause.

ROSSETT PIKE

Region: South **Height:** 2,136 ft **Grid Ref:** NY249076

Rossett Pike provides one of the major routes in or out of Great Langdale in the form of Rossett Gill which is a heavy going route due to the stoniness and steepness although this is now improving due to stone path pitching. The pike isn't that interesting in itself when seen amongst the other jewels of Langdale but it has a great feature nearby in the form of Angle Tarn and provides wonderful views of Mickleden valley and the Langdale Pikes as you move along its heights. Bowfell, being so close, robs the rest of the view. Many will use this way en route to Scafell Pike. The old pony route nearby provides plenty of stories of fact and folklore, especially of smuggling.

The grey-green custodian of Mickleden stands watch,
Guardian of the wide airy expanse of vale below,
Where well-trodden routes to lofty pike and pass,
Whose twisting turning pony track ascent is slow.

From ancient times to the modern here and now,
Mountain folk have left indelible tokens,
The secret devices of herdsman and smugglers,
Where the packwoman's grave lies sleeping, unwoken.

Above Angle Tarn hints of a magical, mystical space,
Where souls rest their weary weather-worn shape,
And refresh the mind's eye in reflected vision of the sky,
Not marred by touch of gusty breath and rippled wake.

ROSTHWAITE FELL (BESSYBOOT)

Region: South **Height:** 2,008 ft **Grid Ref:** NY255188

Not a popular fell as the routes of ascent are few and those that are present are over rough stony ground. Still, I enjoyed my visit. There is Tarn at Leaves and two summits to choose from: Bessyboot and Rosthwaite Cam, with the latter having a fun little scramble to its summit. The views are not the best it must be said, but don't let this put you off a visit. Doves Nest Caves in Comb Gill are worth a look, and fun is had trying to locate them. They should be explored with caution and are out of bounds to your average Lakeland walker.

A lonely fell is Rosthwaite,
Often seen but never climbed,
It's not devoid of interest though,
Hidden Doves Nest Caves to find,
And the Cam a lion without a lamb,
Pleasant Bessyboot the northern height,
Comb Door opens to grander adventures,
The beginning here of Scafell might.

SAIL

Region: North West **Height:** 2,536 ft **Grid Ref:** NY198204

The heathery domed top of Sail has excellent views, but the fell is of little interest other than a stepping stone to the grander prizes of Crag Hill and Eel Crag, the beginning of which blatantly presents itself in the view ahead along the ridge way.

Here few stop,
Hesitate or linger,
Purposely they point,
With firmest finger,
Horseshoe ridge route,
Eel Crag sends,
Sail is so sadly,
A means to an end.

ST SUNDAY CRAG

Region: East **Height:** 2,759 ft **Grid Ref:** NY369135

Some people lovingly tag St Sunday Crag "the Ullswater Fell" for the mountain profile is best seen from the lake's upper reaches. Good views of the fell are often seen by the masses walking along Birkhouse Moor and onto Striding Edge. The very distinctive steep lines make it easy to spot and the fell has always been popular and is now visited more, being part of the Coast to Coast walk. St Sunday Crag is part of the ridge which runs down from the parent fell of Fairfield and looks like a muscular arm to me. The views from the summit are excellent with impressive close up scenery of the vales, and it's fun watching the ants scrambling along and up to Helvellyn.

Where beauty meets remoteness,
On cusp and fringe,
Steep lines soar heavenly,
Shining slender holy lights,
On definition, unique distinctions,
Seeding ambition, aspiring traditions.

SALE FELL

Region: North West **Height:** 1,178 ft **Grid Ref:** NY194297

Sale Fell is a small but popular height that lends itself to gentle walks with beautiful scenery leading through wood and over fell. The summit view is excellent for such a small height and you would almost say you are spoilt with Helvellyn, Skiddaw and even the Galloways Hills showing on a fine day, although Lord's Seat obscures other heights. The water of Bassenthwaite shines nearby.

Wistful wandering ways in Wythop Wood,
Where pleasant platitudes can perchance,
As roe deer appear to promenade, to dance.
Musings, meanderings, meditate on life's happenings,
Ease to restful summit, where the breeze gently sways,
The Skiddaw view unveils, as the roaming sheep graze.

SALLOWS

Region: Far East **Height:** 1,693 ft **Grid Ref:** NY437040

I think it's fair to say that Sallows is a bit of a bland height when compared to others in this region but the walking is easy and the panorama sweeps all round, so that alone makes it worthy of attention. Easy paths from Kentmere or from the road at Ings make this a summit stroll after Sunday lunch along the often grassy knolls that make up Applethwaite Common.

Visited for the varied vista,
Short walk not giving foot a blister,
Western views of Lakeland here relay,
Grand view stretching to Morecambe Bay.

SCAFELL

Region: South **Height:** 3,163 ft **Grid Ref:** NY206064

England's second highest mountain stands proud next to its highest brother and is wonderfully divided and defined by the dropping col of Mickledore. Scafell also has the added drama of being a lot harder to climb for to the north and east the precipitous sides prevent easy access. Broad Stand is really a rock climb, especially in the higher reaches and the usual ascent via Lord's Rake has suffered from rock falls in the last few years, so should be treated with caution. Easier but longer routes head up pleasant paths from the village of Boot. Summit views are excellent and surprisingly different to nearby Scafell Pike because Wastwater and more of the coast are seen.

Mighty Lord and Brother to the King,
Who stands in equal respect and majesty,
Enduring side by side in savage strength,
A towering steadfastness, a beacon of dignity.

Those that worship high ground of reverence,
The hallowed court of Broad Stand – Mickledore,
Are in no doubt as to their minute place,
When seen in midst of nature's war.

Perched high above the rockiest route,
The garnished saxifrage precipices of stone,
Where crags split asunder by thunderous might,
Mark the way to Scafell lofty throne.

SCAFELL PIKE

Region: South **Height:** 3,210 ft **Grid Ref:** NY215072

*England's highest mountain should really need no introduction, but to those
new to its delights my longe poem will hopefully do the job!*

Wastwater frames in deep expanse,
Foundations reflected in silvered pool,
Nature's great work of geological stance,
Shimmering silhouette highest mountain tall,
England's grandest tower in Lakeland so fair,
The path to the loftiest pike a spiritual stair,
Into the very clouds the wind and the rain,
The physical effort, the strain and the pain,
Rewards the soul with grand vision wide,
The heart wells up, great joy it cries.

Scrambling along the vast Scafell range,
The north is Great End, the clues in its name,
Esk Hause to Ill Crag that looks like the moon,
Broad Crag's a challenge, its summit festooned,
Then onto the pike, the highest by far,
Scafell its brother but Broad Stand's a bar!
Slightside most southerly as Lingmell aloof,
All combine majestically, England's vaulted roof,
Diverse in its landscape nature's great work,
Demandingly resolved in reverence please search.

All the jewels that are stored in its crown,
Along the valleys the way up and those down,
Hidden charming tarns, secret places of stone,
Towering on its peak monumental cairned throne,
Three thousand two hundred and ten feet,
From many paths other adventures you'll greet,
Walking from Eskdale, Wasdale so fair,
Borrowdale and Langdale, it's further from there,
Weary travellers, summit exactingly achieved,
Kings of the world so grandly perceived.

SCAR CRAGS

Region: North West **Height:** 2,205 ft **Grid Ref:** NY208206

Scar Crags is rarely climbed for its own sake as there are few feasible paths to do so. But the fell is busy nonetheless, as it makes up part of the long ridge walk of the Coledale Round taking in the major attraction of Eel Crag. The mountain's rugged southern crags fall dramatically down to the beck below and this is the best feature. The rest of the view from the grassy, often muddy, summit is good. The remains of the Lake District's only cobalt mine can be found on the northern slopes – a failed Victorian project by the Keswick Mining Company.

Nature's so blemished,
Harsh violent scar,
Raging rough slope,
Ragged tough mar.

Slanting to southern,
Gothic ugly face,
Dropping darkly down,
Flows Rigg Beck grace.

SCOAT FELL

Region: West **Height:** 2,759 ft **Grid Ref:** NY159113

Scoat Fell has an important role being the hub of a five-spoked wheel of ridges, with paths heading off to Pillar, Wastwater, Red Pike (Wasdale), Haycock and Steeple. In between these spokes are the valleys with Mosedale and Nether Beck the most frequented. As a consequence of this the fell is often climbed as part of the Mosedale Round. The summit is a long stony plateau and has the stone wall known as the Ennerdale Fence running across the east–west heights. This wall sometimes gets in the way of the excellent views but at some points the whole of the Western fells can be observed. A good view of the coves and crags running down off this plateau can be seen from nearby Pillar.

Wild terrain, desolate plateau plain,
The stony Mosedale Round unfolds,
Cliff then follows to darkest hollows,
Where destruction duly reigns.

From cove floor the tower soars,
To heights that carrion aspire,
Walkers come and walkers go,
This ridge way never tires.

SEAT SANDAL

Region: East **Height:** 2,415 ft **Grid Ref:** NY343115

Seat Sandal offers an invitation from nearby Grasmere to the grander heights of the Helvellyn range. The fell has a good recognisable shape and is often admired from below but at the end of the day is a stepping stone nonetheless. The slopes are mainly grassy and easy walking from the west with the view from the summit being excellent. Towards the east the approaches are steep and the view is severely hemmed in by the higher Helvellyn and Fairfield.

Lofty lines from Dunmail Raise,
To plunging depths in darkness shades,
Smooth grass and bracken colour face,
Then fall to tumbled, crumbled rocky waste,
Great Tongue to summit via Grisedale Hause,
Route to higher mountains more often adored.

SEATALLAN

Region: West **Height:** 2,270 ft **Grid Ref:** NY139084

Pronounced Seat-Allan, this fell covers quite a large area of ground but has an unassuming rounded profile compared to the other heights in the district and seems almost bland. A large tumulus marks the grassy summit. The views are restricted by the nearby main range but Scafell and Coniston are seen to good effect. A walk along the ridge to the north will also bring Wastwater into sight. See also the poem for Buckbarrow as these crags really belong to this mountain and are its most prominent feature really, despite Wainwright making them separate entities.

Western wall from Nether Beck,
Shows this mountain's best aspect,
Tongues Gills' route the best to find,
Where the hidden ravines magnificently line.

SEATHWAITE FELL

Region: North West **Height:** 2,073 ft **Grid Ref:** NY227079

This area has long been known as the wettest in England and it has the 3.5 metre annual rainfall records to show it, including the 2009 314.4 mm in twenty-four hours! The fell itself is a rugged and rough mount with a popular bridle path leading to Stockley Bridge and on to the summit via Sty Head Tarn. I also recommend the other route via Sprinkling Tarn via Sty Head or Esk Hause. The views from up top are good especially looking back to Great End and northwards Borrowdale puts on a fair show.

Sprinkling Tarn is aptly named,
For precipitation is the game,
For nowhere else does rainfall more,
Than Seathwaite Fell gill-strewn floor,
Down the streams the torrents flow,
To Derwent River you must go,
Flowing steady from the lake,
Umbrellas here you must take.

SELSIDE PIKE

Region: Far East Height: 2,149 ft Grid Ref: NY487114

The Old Corpse Road on Selside Pike used to carry the dead of Mardale to the nearest church. Now it carries the well-made boots of fell walkers to and from Swindale with the paths spurring off to the large stone-cairned heights. The summit view is confined really to the vista of Haweswater but nonetheless this is quite stunning. This area has quite a bit of history and you can really feel its presence with old ruins here and there, not forgetting the submerged depths of the sunken village of Mardale Green, which paid the price when the lake was raised.

Swindale, such a timid retiring vale,
The Hobgrumble Falls a holy grail,
Dodd Bottom way of ancient tarn bed,
Nabs Crag bows so reverent valley head,
Mardale infamous Old Corpse Road,
Ruins of rocks, strewn old sheepfold,
Walls and enclosures Lakeland type,
All combine the essence of Selside Pike.

SERGEANT MAN

Region: Central **Height:** 2,415 ft **Grid Ref:** NY286089

This central fell is really the second summit of nearby High Raise but with such a prominent rocky cone head certainly deserves its own name. This area is pivotal to the system of ridges that run along these heights. Adventures can be had on the other heights and sights along the way to Sergeant Man, with excellent paths setting out from Grasmere and Langdale taking in some very popular viewpoints. The parent fell gets in the way of the summit views a little but otherwise the panorama is good, especially south.

Attention! Attention! Shouts Sergeant Man,
You are to carry out manoeuvres across my land,
Visit famous tarns along the way,
So much to do, allow a full day,
Tackle me from Grasmere,
Or Dungeon Ghyll,
Explore steep craggy rocks,
Dark ravines give a thrill,
Check out the view,
Standpoint best to the south,
You'll have plenty to say,
Words from your mouth.

SERGEANT'S CRAG

Region: Central **Height:** 1,873 ft **Grid Ref:** NY274114

This fell presents its own very special adventure in the form of Sergeant's Crag. The slopes are very steep as they drop into Langstrath, where fallen rocks abound, and one particular famous landmark in the form of Blea Rock stands proud on a small rise. The summit is usually climbed by following the wall from Eagle Crag or along the southerly flanks where you make your own path to the heights. The views are really good here especially up the valley and towards Bowfell.

Dark shadowy grim rocks frown,
Plunge precipitously down, down, down,
Sharp sudden sheer drama,
Down down, Blea Rock,
Fallen crown split asunder,
Blackmoss Pot rains direction,
Fine day's adventure, recollection.

SHEFFIELD PIKE

Region: East **Height:** 2,215 ft **Grid Ref:** NY368182

Lead and silver were taken from Greenside Mine from the 1750s to the 1960s leaving the ugly marks that mining makes on a mountain. Here on the main feature of Sheffield Pike man has tried to repair his wrongs by turning slag heap into grass banks (to make them safer), but to me it looks a little organised and elsewhere nature over time has done a much better job of repairing the damage, as can be seen on other mountains in the district. The summit views are restricted by the Helvellyn range but on the nearby secondary summit of Heron Pike excellent views of Ullswater unfold.

On Greenside, Glenridding,
As the scars of industrialism slowly fade,
We find slate tips of grass now man-made,
Better to approach from Glencoyne Wood,
Where the aspects are more pleasingly good,
Summit not exciting though certainly worth a hike
For grand view of Ullswater from end Heron Pike.

SHIPMAN KNOTTS

Region: Far East **Height:** 1,926 ft **Grid Ref:** NY472063

Shipman Knotts is one of those lovable little rogues of a fell often climbed on the way to Harter Fell (Mardale) and forms part of the Kentmere horseshoe. Steepness and rough all round are this mountain's true forms. The view from the summit is restricted by the higher fells but the valley of Longsleddale is very well shown.

So well defined in character.

A ragged little rogue of broken rock,
Outcrops burgeon from steep bottom to top,
Boisterous, hard, ungracious, so rough,
Just in case you missed it this mountain is tough!

SILVER HOW

Region: Central **Height:** 1,296 ft **Grid Ref:** NY325066

Sitting above Grasmere village this fell has numerous paths. Add this to the several domed summit tops and you may get a little confused on Silver How. Do not let this put you off though for the scenery in these parts is impressive and this small height has more than its fair share. It is often climbed as part of a longer walk to Blea Rigg and sometimes on to the valley of Great Langdale. The summit, when you eventually find it, is marked by a cairn and excellent views all round can be seen from here, with Grasmere and the valley really catching the eye.

Soft breeze sings gently in the trees,
That cling to pastures' lower slopes,
Here follow the crystal glistening stone,
The rivers of descending waterfalls,
Flowing fast on fringe of rocky steps,
Routes rising to heights' prominent undulations,
The pleasant crowned grass-topped elevations,
Panorama of Grasmere, richest Lakeland scene,
Ah, sweet sylvan shades of the Silver How dream.

SKIDDAW

Region: North Height: 3,054 ft Grid Ref: NY260290

The town of Keswick has an abundance of riches surrounding it, too many to name here in this short paragraph. One of these is Skiddaw, the 4th highest mountain in England. Despite its grand height the fell is one of the easiest to climb with well-marked paths from Keswick town's lower height of Latrigg, which are ideal for the first timer or the day tripper who wants to get a taste of mountains. A more exciting approach for the more experienced is from Longside Edge following the ridge up Ullock Pike. The windy summit has many tops, High Man being the true zenith, and the views from all of these are truly excellent.

Benevolent green giant escapes from the norm,
Sudden steepness shapes your elegant form,
It's hard to imagine the heights that be,
Were once deposits in the long lost sea,
Skiddaw is old aged beyond compare,
Friend, wise mentor to those that live there,
The undulating ridge half a mile long,
Where summit air's brisk, broad and strong,
Whip Arctic winds from face to face,
The top in harsh weather is a cruel, cruel place.

SKIDDAW LITTLE MAN

Region: North **Height:** 2,838 ft **Grid Ref:** NY266277

If ever a mountain was wrongly named it is this one, for its current title gives the wrong impression totally. It is an independent fell and grand amongst most of its Lake District peers. Yes, Skiddaw nearby stands that much taller but Little Man, as it is often shown on maps, has a distinct advantage. The curved upward southern slope creates a truly wonderful viewing platform.

There is nothing diminutive about this place,
This lofty fell appeals to all variety of tastes,
Many climbers, scramblers, walkers galore,
Who often set out from the Millbeck floor,
Earn the reverend sights of presented panorama,
And aspect of nature's opened loving drama,
Southern view fantastical, some say Lakeland best,
Your eyes will not be drawn to the North, East or West.

SLIGHT SIDE

Region: South **Height:** 2,500 ft **Grid Ref:** NY209050

This fell provides a wonderful terminal point on the southern ridge of the Scafell range and is usually ascended from beautiful Eskdale. The summit has a fine pointed rocky peak and provides an excellent platform for a truly stunning view towards the coast. Be careful with your map reading as Long Green is very often mistaken for Slight Side despite them being nearly a mile apart.

Rise! Rise! Rise! To the grand conclusion,
Along the crag-strewn terrace to the top,
For here lies Slight Side's shapely summit,
And more than briefly here will you stop,
For Westward Ho! Your gaze will draw,
Down majestic foothills and valleys seen,
Flow of river, sweeping vale will guide you,
To the shining silvered glass of sea.

SOUR HOWES

Region: Far East **Height:** 1,585 ft **Grid Ref:** NY427032

Here on Applethwaite Common lie two fells, Sallows and Sour Howes, both providing easy walking country on grassy knolls. The real interest here is in the views on offer and the eye is undoubtedly drawn to Windermere nearby.

This mount more famous for its view,
The place itself, a grassy hummock pew,
Westward waters the stunning sight goes,
A Sunday stroll, a walk for restless toes.

SOUTHER FELL

Region: North **Height:** 1,713 ft **Grid Ref:** NY355292

This region is seen as a bit of a geological rarity as this fell is surrounded on three sides by a river which runs six miles around its slopes. In truth, following its course would be more interesting than scaling the heights if was not because of the really good views that loom round the corner of the nearby parent fell of Blencathra.

Rivers, waters bound,

Surrounding Souther slopes,

Lonely bridges found,

Breaching Glenderamackin hopes.

STARLING DODD

Region: West Height: 2,077 ft Grid Ref: NY142158

The wealth of beauty in the Western fells is well known but Starling Dodd does not count itself amongst them. This average height is hidden by two valleys and is not often seen, let alone climbed. Those who make an effort, in all fairness are rewarded with good views but if you have made the climb directly then wet muddy feet from the many bogs will be your doom. Best to approach indirectly along the ridges. It's interesting to note that Wainwright walkers often save this fell for their 214 finale – it was the last one Alfred climbed when researching his famous guides.

Subtle, modest, unassuming type,
Bland steep slopes lead to grassy heights,
Hidden up two valleys, so often not seen,
A place only summit baggers have faithfully been.

STEEL FELL

Region: Central Height: 1,814 ft Grid Ref: NY319112

Steel Fell is often seen from the main artery road of the A591 which runs up through the centre of the Lake District. The steep slopes catch the eye although not many know the fell's name. Ascents from Steel End at the southern end of Thirlmere are quite common as is the way from Town Head near Grasmere. A very direct route from the roadside path at Dunmail Raise near the ancient cairn, heads virtually straight up to the heights. The good views here lead naturally north to Blencathra and south to Coniston.

Rough walls surround scree-littered slopes,
The formidable flanks of Steel Fell rise,
Catching the eye from highway below,
The flanks so steep make progress slow.

If Dunmail King indeed lies at Dunmail Raise,
What ill fate dealt at modern hand of man?
Old Cairn Royal holds court each day,
In the middle of the busy dual carriageway!

STEEL KNOTTS

Region: Far East **Height:** 1,417 ft **Grid Ref:** NY440181

In between the valleys of Fusedale and Martindale a ridge runs north to south and here we find Steel Knotts, a small height with a lot of character. Often climbed from Howtown, with many arriving via the Ullswater ferry, the ridge provides a really nice walk with an exciting little scramble to the summit which has its own name. The views here are really good, especially of Martindale and along the grand heights of Helvellyn.

Junior heights delight
In true
Eccentric rocky might,
Named fondly
Pikeawassa summit tor,
Legend laid,
Fine summit soars.

STEEPLE

Region: West **Height:** 2,687 ft **Grid Ref:** NY157116

The sharp peak of Steeple is so well named with hardly room for a summit cairn at its pointed top. This prominent profile makes it easily recognisable and also makes it a "must do" ascent. Many rise to the challenge. The fell is often walked in conjunction with Pillar and other nearby mountains but a direct ascent from Ennerdale, through the forest, is equally popular. The views are a little bit restricted by higher fells but what is on offer is a very fine vista of the valley and more intimately the cliffs of Mirk Cove.

Let me introduce you to a fell called Steeple,
Named correctly and loved by people,
Proud, profound, prominent, pointed peak,
The view from the summit a great thrill to seek,
Climbed from the wooded Ennerdale floor,
Gap through the plantation, the forested door

STONE ARTHUR

Region: East **Height:** 1,650 ft **Grid Ref:** NY348093

Stone Arthur is the lower part of the ridge leading to Great Rigg and is an excellent viewpoint. Often pathless, ascents from Grasmere can be made up the steep slopes, sometimes through thick gorse or by following ways up Greenhead or Tongue gills. These add water to the River Rothay which flows through the village and into Grasmere.

Ruined castle-like tor,
Called aptly Stone Arthur,
No sword found in the stone,
If that's what you're after,
Just graceful waters show,
Vista gem of Easedale Tarn,
And William speaks on the wind
Whispering the Waggoner yarn.

STYBARROW DODD

Region: East **Height:** 2,766 ft **Grid Ref:** NY343189

Those that walk the main ridge of the Helvellyn range or those on the round of the Deepdale Dodds will pass by Stybarrow Dodd. The many that use Sticks Pass will just glance at the grassy slopes from a distance normally making a beeline for Helvellyn or the villages of Legburthwhaite and Glenridding found at either end of this walkers' highway. Summits (there are two) show little in the way of rock but the views are really excellent as all the major ranges are on display. When I last approached from the west I left the main path – as is often my way when water is at hand – and followed the way up Stanah Gill. It's quite beautiful in places.

Eastwards falls to Ullswater shores,
Westward for Stanah Gill I implore,
The many over Sticks Pass they roam,
Though few will call at Stybarrow Dodd home,
Where winds whip wild on slopes of verdant grass,
Here vista displayed, the memory will last.

SWIRL HOW

Region: South **Height:** 2,631 ft **Grid Ref:** NY273006

Swirl How is a major player in the Coniston range with ridges leading to other fells in all major directions. Many, though not all, will walk the heights via the Old Man as routes up from Little Langdale are also increasing in popularity. The very windy, stony summit is marked by a really good cairn from which the views are excellent. So keep an eye out for the Isle of Man and even the Pennines on a clear day, once you have drawn your gaze away from the nearby legion of fells.

North, East, South and West your ridges range,
Radiating in geological splendid symmetry,
The distant silhouette of prominent profile,
Leaves man in no doubt of lauded vicinity.

For here lies the sharp breaking summit,
Where winds torment peak of Swirl How mortar,
Here waters fall to Rivers Brathay and Duddon
And breathe life into still Coniston Water.

TARN CRAG (EASEDALE)

Region: Central **Height:** 1,808 ft **Grid Ref:** NY301093

Tarn Crag can be seen dominating the northern skyline from the shore of the very beautiful Easedale Tarn, the walk to which is really a "must do" for every visitor to the Lake District. If this walk can be incorporated into a visit to this fell's summit all the better, for you will be rewarded with an excellent view and a little surprise just beyond.

Climb the well-worn steps to Sour Milk Gill,
Then on to Easedale postcard thrill,
Follow shoreline round to the right,
And take the old path to Tarn Crag heights.

Though not many walkers here you'll find,
The climb is rewarded with a view that's fine
And a hidden gem beyond the rugged top,
Codale Tarn is a well-worthy stop.

TARN CRAG (LONGSLEDDALE)

Region: Far East **Height:** 2,178 ft **Grid Ref:** NY488078

In truth Tarn Crag is on the outskirts of Lakeland and in this case suffers a little for it, for the views are not best of the mountains although towards Morecambe Bay a fine vista is seen. The more worthy Buckbarrow Crag is nearby and Tarn Crag is often "bagged" when a visit is made here. One of the four infamous unusually constructed Haweswater survey pillars can be found here.

This place is on the Lakeland verge,
For slovenly slopes in Shap Fells merge,
Another Wainwright summit to earnestly bag,
And worth the visit for Buckbarrow Crag.

THORNTHWAITE CRAG

Region: Far East **Height:** 2,572 ft **Grid Ref:** NY432101

A true focal point, for Thornthwaite Crag guards the head of several valleys and it is only right that the summit is marked by the stone beacon that stands so tall. The Roman road of High Street crosses the summit plateau (making a straight line for the fell of the same name), a grassy top with an important crossroad of paths. The views here are good and very changeable as you walk around the edge of the summit.

From miles around many have sought token,
Tall pillar stones of Thornthwaite Beacon,
Here stand summit and landmark tower,
Forthright statement of nature's power,
Valleys Troutbeck, Threshthwaite here tolled,
Hayeswater and Kentmere dutifully unfold.

THUNACAR KNOTT

Region: Central **Height:** 2,372 ft **Grid Ref:** NY279079

The interesting title might excite many into thinking that this is a significant place. Sadly it is not, as for starters the summit is barely discernible, a slight rise in the moorland. Add this to the fell being surrounded by the gems of Langdale and you really have a "lose lose" situation. Visitors here do in all truth get a good westerly view but the majority of walkers are mainly summit baggers. You only have to ask and they will say "Just another tick on the way to 214!"

Poor old Thunacar Knott,
Uninspiring mountain is your lot,
Of all the jewels in Langdale so fair,
Unphotogenic your cupboard bare,
The spacious sheepwalks seem all the same,
The best thing about you is your name!

TROUTBECK TONGUE

Region: Far East **Height:** 1,194 ft **Grid Ref:** NY422064

The small height of Troutbeck Tongue sits in Troutbeck Park and although small in nature puts up a bold defence of its summit heights. A short steep but fun walk-come-scramble begins at Troutbeck Farm, once owned by Beatrix Potter and now of course the property of the National Trust. The view from up here is dominated by England's longest lake.

From very modest wedge no places to slip,
Except from The Tongue's rocky rib tip,
This enigmatic height is a fun Sunday climb,
With great southern views along Windermere lines.

ULLOCK PIKE

Region: North **Height:** 2,270 ft **Grid Ref:** NY244287

Ullock Pike is an exciting start for many to the northern prize of Skiddaw and is part of what is regarded as one of the best ridge walks in the district. This route also takes in Long Side and Carl Side on the way to the grander height and offers good views and rock edge drama almost all the way. The fell has a carpet of fine heather for the most part although an unusual rock formation that goes by the name of Watches stands out amongst the grass. It looks a bit like a man-made stone circle but is entirely natural.

There is a pleasant little hike,
Along the edge up Ullock Pike,
From Ravenstone or Barkbeth starts,
You'll take this summit close to heart,
From here vaulted view really delivers,
Bassenthwaite Lake and Derwent River.

ULLSCARF

Region: Central **Height:** 2,382 ft **Grid Ref:** NY292122

Ullscarf really does have its own unique style, shall we say, for it is defended for the most part by crags on its lower slopes that then rise to rather bland grassy summit slopes. The view from here is really good but on a misty day care should be taken for the area is wide and this main ridge of the Central fells very often changes direction. You will find few paths or cairns hereabouts. The Coast to Coast walk skirts Greenup valley and by Lining Crag, the fell's most recognisable feature.

This mountain is the wrong way round,
Its grass pastures should be near ground,
Fierce crags should sit proud on summit top,
Upside down mountain, a strange what-not,
From these verdant heights the view is grand,
Showing North and West, fine looking fell bands.

WALLA CRAG

Region: Central **Height:** 1,243 ft **Grid Ref:** NY276212

Well loved is Walla Crag and not without good reason is this little gem adored. The fell's feet stand on the shore of Derwentwater and then rise steeply up a terminal cliff face. This area is heavily wooded almost all the way to the top and lovely paths run from here or from Keswick. A route also runs from the summit to Bleaberry Fell, which like Walla Crag has really stunning views. Nearby Falcon Crag is very popular amongst rock climbers.

Unassailable or so you seem,
But truth beholds in mine eye,
Yours is all that's best in beauty,
Encompassing true romantic forms,
In many resplendent rugged faces,
Which the sunlight gently graces,
Seen from sweetest Derwentwater shores,
Your rocks fall fast to wooded floors.

WANDOPE

Region: North West **Height:** 2,533 ft **Grid Ref:** NY188197

Wandope is a well-used fell but quite often the interesting Addacomb Hole is not noticed by walkers on the way to the grander heights of the Grasmoor–Causey Pike ridge. This hanging valley, almost symmetrical in shape, creates a huge crater with its front wall nearly 700 feet high and is certainly worth the extra effort of a visit. The summit in comparison is a gentle grass slope with excellent views. The north is blocked by Grasmoor; however, Scafell and its fellows put on a glorious show from here.

There is a place often missed, true mountain soul,
Grand profound hollow they call Addacomb Hole,
As most urgent walkers head magnetic to heights,
Eel Crag, Grasmoor and Whiteless Pike.

Pause for a moment, stand and stare,
This intense hanging valley so high in the air,
Visit the stream where it issues supreme,
Where white waters dance, cascading so keen.

WANSFELL

Region: East **Height:** 1,597 ft **Grid Ref:** NY403051

At the end of the long ridge of Caudale Moor near the town of Ambleside you can find Wansfell. This fell's true summit is not the most exciting place to visit but not all is lost by a long chalk! On its lower heights can be found several charming and well-visited places in the form of crags, woods and strong waters. The poem will tell you more. The summit, or I should say summits, as a more interesting viewing platform can be found on the secondary height of Wansfell Pike, provides good views of Lake Windermere.

For Wansfell summit there is little will,
It has no appeal or allure to thrill,
Though on its slopes there's much to like,
With the Windermere view from the pike,
And Ambleside visitors have often stood,
On Jenkins Crag in Skelghyll Wood,
Here the panorama widely westwards spans,
From Loughrigg Fell to Coniston Old Man,
Oh please don't forget Stock Ghyll Force,
This fervent stream goes fully the course.

WATSON'S DODD

Region: East **Height:** 2,589 ft **Grid Ref:** NY336196

Watson's Dodd for the most part is a pleasant but unassuming fell amongst the grandees of the Helvellyn range. One noted feature though is the literally famous Castle Rock, a crag on its lower slopes, well named, stunningly picturesque and referred to by Walter Scott in his The Bridal of Triermain. *The summit by comparison is a grass plain and is often reached by those walking the main ridge. The views up here are really good though in all directions. If you want to do a rare direct ascent then I can recommend following the scramble up the water course or the walk on the right shoulder up Mill Gill ravine, although paths are few.*

Memories of Watson's Dodd remain,
For the Castle Rock of Triermain,
A short ascent to this keep of stone,
The Vale of St John where eyes will roam,

Then if you wish to scale the heights,
Follow Mill Gill, a ravine delight,
This scramble for some is worth a look,
Though not often mentioned in many books.

WETHER HILL

Region: Far East **Height:** 2,211 ft **Grid Ref:** NY456167

Rock gives way to grass as the Far Eastern fells drop to the lesser ridges in the north. Wether Hill carries the Roman High Street slightly below the summit where good views of the Helvellyn range and the Pennines put on a show of opposite directions. Often climbed from the beautiful valleys of Fusedale or Martindale, in truth these valleys are of more interest than the grassy plains above. Ancient stone circles and other such works can be found in several places in this area.

Broad grassy mounds on ridge prevail,
As High Street range begins to fail,
Secluded slopes sprawl wide descending,
Becks gain force, water crescendoing.

Ancient cairns mark man's ancestors,
Solitary standing stones with spiritual senses,
Here the valleys not the high mountains,
Hold the joy of nature's blessed fountain.

WETHERLAM

Region: South **Height:** 2,502 ft **Grid Ref:** NY288011

Standing apart from the main Coniston ridge, Wetherlam is often approached from the nearby windy Swirl How and is part of the round popular on this range which begins with an ascent of the Old Man. The slopes on this fell (as are most in this region) are littered with small old copper and slate mines, mainly Victorian in age. Interest in exploring these old workings is on the rise and good fun can be had doing so. But none should be entered as the shafts collapse from time to time!

The mighty mass of Wetherlam holds upright,
A monument to the futility of man's endeavour,
For the harsh pitting, piercing and pummelling,
Cannot bring this giant down to earth,
Nor can human industry mar marvellous worth,
For long after the life of mortal man,
This mountain will prevail and firmly stand.

WHIN RIGG

Region: South **Height:** 1,755 ft **Grid Ref:** NY151034

The drama of Wastwater Screes is seen in full evidence here at Whin Rigg, this fell being a continuation of the ridge from Illgill Head. Whilst the Screes rightly take all the plaudits another noted feature is Greathall Gill as many will ascend this beautiful ravine on their way to the heights. The summit is all about the precipitous view downwards!

A desolate scene set of savage imagery
For fallen flank of mountainside,
Shows proud scar on shattered ridge,
The dark chasms haunt and hypnotise,
Holding your gaze in grey Gothic tombs,
Softened, tempered by nature's blend,
In rich deep mirrored wooded waters end.

WHINLATTER

Region: North West **Height:** 1,722 ft **Grid Ref:** NY197249

Whinlatter is a popular place with its own visitor centre which includes impressive mountain bike trails running through the large forest, and other adventurous attractions. The fell is easily climbed and provides lovely paths in the woods. The summit does not have the best views of Lakeland, it must be said, with the exception of Hopegill Head. But westerly along the undulating heights the Solway Firth and Scotland come into view.

Many have found,
Ways along road,
True mountain pass,
Places to roam,
Routes through forest,
Head to heights,
Rolling green plateau,
Reveals Northern lights.

WHITE SIDE

Region: East **Height:** 2,831 ft **Grid Ref:** NY337166

White Side runs down from the heights of Helvellyn along the main north–south range but stills remains at a respectable altitude and provides good views from the broad grassy summit. The fell gets its name from the white quartz running through the more dramatic rocky eastern slopes which is in keeping with the region's geology and topography, the western slopes being tame as they slope down to Thirlmere. Keppel Cove is situated on the eastern slopes and is the home of the country's first hydro-electric dam which now lies in ruins. The dam burst back in 1927 wrecking the village of Glenridding below.

Here white quartz splashed randomly on rock,
Keppel Cove showing this mountain's true stock,
With silent recesses, here wind turns you pale,
Falling fast abruptly to wide, wide vale,
There lies the smashed dam, the shadowed tarn,
Where water once ravaged doing great harm.

WHITELESS PIKE

Region: North West **Height:** 2,165 ft **Grid Ref:** NY180189

Buttermere village is the perfect starting point for Whiteless Pike and this fell's panorama opens up as you climb Whiteless Breast to the summit, the view from which is really good with most major Lakeland fells showing well, along with the local waters. Many walkers will continue along this ridge to Wandope and then onto the delights of Crag Hill.

Rewarding Buttermere hike,
Raising Whiteless Pike
Wide uplifted scene,
Panorama sublime supreme,
Valleys show below,
Distant horizon grows.

WHITESIDE

Region: North West **Height:** 2,359 ft **Grid Ref:** NY175221

Whiteside is a fine adventure, a mountain of character, and lies on the westerly end of the excellent Hopegill Head to Grisedale Pike ridge, one of the best walks in this region. There is plenty to see along the way with rock features a plenty in the form of crag and buttress. Views are changeable but for the most are really good especially to the north and west. The fell has three summits no less, with Whiteside, Gasgale Crags and the true summit of East Top. Whiteside, however, is considered the "Wainwright" for you official summit baggers.

Much to admire much to adore,
From mountain high to valley floor,
Buttresses many grand Dodd and Penn,
Range round western heights to Whiteside End,
Paths along valley, rough Gasgale Gill,
To Whin Ben route giving crag edge thrill,
Top views from summits target coastal plain
High up to Scotland's sights can be claimed.

YEWBARROW

Region: West **Height:** 2,060 ft **Grid Ref:** NY173084

Yewbarrow may be one of the lesser heights in the Wasdale Head region but it should not be taken on lightly, as some of the main ascents can mean some scrambling in places. Such is the nature of this fine fell for the summit areas rise up from the pastures below to steep crag and crevice. Some routes can be found to circumvent this, so study the map and climb in good weather. The summit is grass which surprised me after the rockiest of ascents but the biggest surprise was the view this fabulous platform gives – an uninterrupted panorama all round with Great Gable and the Scafell range the stars. By the way, I thought I'd get a limerick in before the last poem!

There once was a fell called Yewbarrow,
That had dangerous ascents that could harrow,
From the easy pastures before,
You stand by Great Door
Where the ridge extends and the crest narrows.

YOKE

Region: Far East **Height:** 2,316 ft **Grid Ref:** NY437067

So onto my final poem as far as the Wainwrights are concerned, a couple of years work behind me. Yoke lies between two valleys and like other Lake District fells presents two opposing faces. One of these presents the 300-foot Rainsborrow Crag, a training ground for climbers. Down in the valley the large boulder of Brock Stone (sometimes called Badger Rock) provides initial practice for the novices. This fell is included in the Kentmere Horseshoe but is not one of the most exciting; the true drama heads towards Harter Fell (Mardale) and Ill Bell.

In Troutbeck valley you'll receive,
A sight of Yoke that can deceive,
Don't be fooled, lots can be found,
Than what looks like a grassy mound.

For from Kentmere you will see what's true,
Knott and crag fill vastly changed view,
Here climbing novices learn their craft's bones,
Up Rainsborrow Crag and warm.

LASTLY SOME THANKS.

So there you have my Wainwrights In Verse 214 poems. The work has been up hill in some regard which is apt seeing as this book is about climbing mountains but such is life and the journey I have been on to get to this finished stage has quite frankly been the making of me as a person.

Whatever the outcome or however well received or not this book becomes I actually saw something through the end that was totally my own making, my own 'Magnus Opus' if you like.

I have had some wonderful adventures too now that have drowned out the darker times I experienced which initially actually lead to the birth of this book.

Some thought I was mad, some said it could not be done, others that a poetry book would never make any money. None of this really bothered me or gave me doubts I ploughed on regardless because of my passion and love for the fells.

I'd really like to thank Yve Pope for shouting at me and keeping me going!

Thanks to Liz Lemal for her work with some of the editing and proof reading.

Also thanks to all those that supported me on my social media sites, the comments, the likes and the shares.

I have met and will continue to meet fellow adventures out on the fells and at the various bars for a trophy pint or two, so if you see me do come say Hello!

Made in the USA
Charleston, SC
22 February 2015